ISRAEL/PALESTINE

The Quest for Dialogue

Haim Gordon and Rivca Gordon,
Editors

ORBIS BOOKS

Maryknoll, New York 10545

The Catholic Foreign Mission Society of America (Maryknoll) recruits and trains people for overseas missionary service. Through Orbis Books, Maryknoll aims to foster the international dialogue that is essential to mission. The books published, however, reflect the opinions of their authors and are not meant to represent the official position of the society.

Library of Congress Cataloging-in-Publication Data

Israel/Palestine: the quest for dialogue / Haim Gordon and Rivca
    Gordon, editors.
        p.   cm.
    ISBN 0-88344-731-2
    1. Jewish-Arab relations—1973-   2. National characteristics,
Israeli.   3. Palestinian Arabs—Politics and government.
I. Gordon, Hayim.   II. Gordon, Rivca.
DS119.7.I8262   1991
956—dc20   90-26348
                                                      CIP

vi   *Contents*

*For Nitzan, Mor, Neve, Omri, Dalit, Oshrat
we hope that you will live in a world of dialogue*

Contents

v

Introduction

HAIM GORDON AND RIVCA GORDON

In the melee of conflicting statements and aggressive exchanges emerging from the Middle East for many decades, the voices of those persons who for years have been working for Israeli-Palestinian dialogue have often been unheard. That was a major reason we initiated this book—to provide a platform for some of those Palestinians and Israelis whose dedicated and diligent work for dialogue has been frequently ignored by the media and by their fellow residents of this part of the world. A second reason was to show some of the difficult problems these workers for dialogue face. And a final reason was to confront and to reject the enmity between Israelis and Palestinians, and to suggest that we can live in this area of the world as peaceful neighbors.

We believe that four major reasons underlie the fact that Israelis and Palestinians who work for dialogue have been much too frequently ignored. First, speakers for dialogue can only rarely engage in the kind of volatile and ostentatious rhetoric that often arouses the enthusiasm of the masses. They will never attempt to play upon listeners' hidden fears, suppressed anxiety, flight from anguish, mediocre beliefs, or restrained hatred of others. Workers for dialogue will refuse to link themselves to any form of chauvinism, jingoism, fatalism, or fanaticism, because all these approaches eclipse and frequently oppress the personal freedom necessary for genuine dialogue to emerge. In other words, since dialogue is based on freedom, it requires that one firmly reject the pernicious common fare provided by many of the banal leaders in this area of the world to their ardent

1

followers. Let us say it categorically. Masses of people in the Middle East daily ingest the common fare of jingoism, chauvinism, fanaticism, and fatalism that their mediocre leaders proffer; they delight in the feasts of aroused hostility and pompous antagonism concocted from different manners of expressing hatred. They forcefully reject whoever refuses to partake in this witch's feast.

Second, since workers for dialogue appeal to one's freedom, they make difficult demands upon their partners in dialogue, their listeners. Most prominent is the demand that one listen carefully to the voices of persons who are often considered by one's milieu to be one's odious enemies, the embodiments of evil. After such listening the worker for dialogue demands that the listener consider what has been said and relate to it honestly, without in any way attempting to manipulate the other person or the conversation. In the Middle East these demands often seem to be totally out of place. Manipulation and violence are very much accepted as the only correct and sane manners of dealing with a person considered to be an enemy. (In large sections of the Middle East violence is the only acceptable response to one's honor being abused.) Thus the simple demand that one listen carefully to one's so-called enemy and respond honestly and not manipulatively can be threatening—because it includes an implicit demand to alter one's established Weltanschauung, or, even more, to change one's being-in-the-world. No wonder that many Jews and Arabs, residents of the Middle East, ignore the voices of workers for dialogue.

Third, the worker for dialogue often seems to stutter, and not because of a speaking defect. Speakers for dialogue seem to repeat accepted clichés and promote a mode of behavior that most intellectuals and politicians proudly declare they happily support. Lately, dialogue, like motherhood and apple pie, has become something no one would openly reject. Even cruel fanatics of evil can list themselves as promoters of dialogue. Thus, a savage instigator of genocide like Pol Pot would probably say that he supports dialogue. (He may even have already said it.) The same is probably true of Iraq's Saddam Hussein. Clearly the concept of dialogue has often been stretched to include almost all modes of verbal interaction. Consequently, the worker for dialogue must find new ways to distinguish between genuine dialogue and manipulative negotiations, cocktail party interchanges, or other verbal interactions that in the minds of many have often usurped genuine dialogue. One such manner of distinguishing is by seeking new expressions or terms that can appeal to an existential level in the life of one's listeners, not attainable by manipulatory rhetoric. (Martin Buber's "I-Thou" comes to mind.) But such expressions are hard to come by, and their meaning is often difficult to convey. Hence the impression that the worker for dialogue stutters, or is repeating well-known clichés. The reader shall encounter such stuttering quite often in the following pages.

Fourth, the worker for dialogue readily admits that dialogue is a long arduous process. Genuine dialogue develops dialectically; it takes time. In the process of engaging in dialogue one must slowly build the mutual trust necessary for a deeper level of dialogue. But most people, most Jews and Arabs in this area of the world, are unwilling to wait; they want a quick, pointed decision; they demand an immediate solution to their pressing problem. Consequently, they view dialogue as an exercise in futility and purposely ignore the worker for dialogue.

Despite their often being ignored, and at times even despised by some of their compatriots, a group of dedicated Jewish and Arab men and women have for years worked for dialogue. The fact that they decided to contribute their insights, their beliefs, their hopes, their sufferings, their fears, their dreams, their frustrations — and yes, their clichés and their stutterings — to this volume only speaks for their devotion and fortitude. It also reveals a human component of the sad situation in Israel and the occupied territories that should be better known. In this area well-known for terrorism, brutality, violence, killings, beatings, jingoism, chauvinism, fanaticism — in this area there are courageous persons who firmly speak out for mutual trust and for Israeli-Palestinian dialogue. These persons, commonplace or unique as their message may be, deserve to be heard.

We should perhaps immediately add that we wanted the voices of persons working for dialogue in Israel and Palestine to be heard, even if what many of these voices had to say would often make us, as Jews, be ashamed of some of our country's long-established policies. These policies have for more than twenty years deliberately exploited and oppressed the mass of Palestinians living under Israeli occupation on the West Bank and in the Gaza Strip. By denying these Palestinians all political rights and many civil rights, by not allowing industries to be developed in the occupied territories, by forcefully taking land away from Arabs and giving it to Jews, by using the Israel Security Service to intimidate any Palestinian who opposed this official policy, by allowing military rule to be the law of the land for more than two decades—by these draconian decrees and dehumanizing policies, Israeli policy-makers have attempted to mold most of the Palestinians into a mass of subjugated and often pulverized human beings. In Karl Marx's terms, they have made every attempt to relegate Palestinians in the occupied territories to the level of *Lumpenproletariat.* Furthermore, during the almost quarter-century of oppressing and exploiting Palestinians, of forcing them to live under tyrannical military rule, large numbers of Jews in Israel have begun to think of racism against Arabs as a legitimate policy. For these Jewish racists, speaking with Palestinians, listening to them attentively, relating to them personally, engaging in dialogue with them, is an act of betrayal.

The Jewish population in Israel also prefers to overlook many brutal facts that are outcomes of our ongoing military occupation and of our policies of oppressing the residents of the West Bank and the Gaza Strip. In the Gaza Strip, for instance, almost five hundred thousand Palestinians live in squalid refugee camps. They have no sanitary facilities, their shacks are small and crowded together; in short, conditions are often appalling and dehumanizing. Many of these refugees live off a U.N. daily food allowance; many others find work in Israel as underpaid day laborers. But according to official Israeli policy, these refugees are an Arab problem, a U.N. problem, certainly not a problem that the Israeli government needs to address. In other words, Israel is willing to rule the Gaza Strip as it has done for more than twenty years, but is not willing to cope with the existential problems of the refugees residing there. Perhaps we should add that according to U.N. statistics the Gaza Strip is the most densely populated area on earth.

Not only Palestinian refugees have suffered from the Israeli occupation. The Palestinian intellectuals who have participated in this book are not refugees. But they have all been interrogated, jailed, refused permission to travel, censured when they wish to write and to speak out. They live under the threat of being called up by the Israel Security Service and being charged with some violation of Israel's draconian military laws.

While criticizing the ongoing Israeli oppression of the Palestinians, we would be much too naive if we denied the fact that for more than four decades many Palestinians and Israelis have often viewed each other as bitter enemies, violently inflicting much suffering on each other, quite often killing innocent people. The ongoing struggle for the land upon which both nations reside has led to many atrocious deeds. No side — neither the Palestinians nor the Israelis — is free from guilt. Furthermore, in this struggle Palestinian terrorism and Israeli oppression seem to have been linked together in a symbiotic relationship that has sanctioned cruelty and violence, and nurtured and supported the chauvinism, jingoism, fanaticism, and fatalism mentioned above. The need to counter these adverse trends is the thrust of this book. Dialogue, we believe, is an enhancing manner of coping with such long-lasting enmity.

No. We have no illusions. Differences will remain, friendships may not arise, animosity will not disappear, disagreements may deepen. However, if dialogue prevails, the manner of coping with these attitudes and problems will be based on the mutual respect that arises in the dialogical relationship.

Israel's peace treaty with Egypt is a case in point. Even today both Israelis and Egyptians call the relationship between the two countries a cold peace. Indeed, cultural, religious, economic, social, and political differences between Israel and Egypt have hardly been addressed in the twelve years of peace. There have been very few attempts to initiate mutual economic or social projects. There has been very little authentic interaction between Israelis and Egyptians. Not a few Egyptians still despise Israelis and let Israeli tourists know their feelings; almost no Egyptian tourists visit Israel. And yet, when pressing political differences arise between Egypt and Israel, they are resolved in an atmosphere of negotiation and at times of dialogue. The peace treaty signed between Egypt and Israel more than a decade ago has led both nations to understand that they can live as neighbors without active hostilities. Thus, dialogue between Israelis and Palestinians need not necessarily lead to friendship. At least there is a recognition on both sides of the rights of one's partner to live in political freedom, without the threat of war or oppression.

When we initiated this book we also wanted to learn more about our fellow workers for dialogue. As indicated, working for dialogue in the Middle East is quite a lonely endeavor. One is quite often ignored or rejected by one's milieu, one is frequently swimming against the stream. But we did not foresee the many difficulties demanded by editing this book. The odyssey of enlisting participants for this book, convincing them to write, and preparing the book for publication was fascinating, frustrating, at times frightening, and also quite exhausting. Many meetings, phone calls, discussions, revisions, clarifications were needed — all this during a period when the *intifada*, the Palestinian uprising, with its curfews, strikes, and ongoing violence, was a daily fact of life in Palestinian villages, towns, and cities, and also in many sections of Jerusalem.

We were stubborn, and probably naive or stupid. We entered neighborhoods where Jews had recently been knived and stoned by Palestinians. We set up meetings with Palestinians in places that would not arouse suspicion of the Israel Security Service. We asked Palestinians to consult with us, knowing that such a rendezvous might endanger them. We were quite often aggravated and peeved — at ourselves for undertaking such a frustrating and dangerous odyssey, at the ongoing brutality of the Israeli-Palestinian conflict, which showed no signs of reaching a peaceful solution, at the myopic, cruel response of our government to the Palestinian uprising and to the wish of the Palestinian leadership to engage in dialogue, at our authors when they failed to meet deadlines. Quite a few times we felt that our task was worthy, for instance, when we finally received an article and found that it exceeded our expectations. This entire process taught us, as editors, some important lessons, which we believe the reader should keep in mind.

Perhaps the most important lesson was one that we had repeatedly learned during our many years of working for dialogue, but it was reaffirmed through meaningful personal encounters with the authors in this book. We can formulate the lesson thus. Even during this harsh period of the *intifada*, which is characterized by daily acts of violence, on this land of Israel-Palestine, which is holy to the three monotheistic faiths, live tens of thousands of Israelis and Palestinians who firmly desire to live in peace with each other, who are willing to engage in dialogue, who wish to pursue their lives and faiths without infringing upon the freedom of others. Indeed, the difficult encounters and the exhausting toil that resulted in this book made us firmer in our belief that Jerusalem, as a city that is holy to Judaism, Christianity, and Islam can and should become a center for interfaith dialogue. We believe that many of the inhabitants of this city, perhaps even its silent majority, are pro-dialogue.

We say all this despite many facts that seemingly contradict us, such as the Israeli government's cynical attempt to take over part of the Christian quarter in Jerusalem, or the fact that the Israeli police allow right-wing Jews to conduct pogroms against Arabs in Arab sections of Jerusalem. We say it despite large Palestinian demonstrations in favor of Saddam Hussein and his evil regime, and the repeated killing of innocent Jews by Palestinian terrorists. We say it because we believe that many Israelis and Palestinians prefer dialogue to violence. These people know that in this part of the world there does not seem to be a third alternative.

But this lesson has an underside that must not be overlooked. What frequently happens in the Middle East is that persons who are pro-dialogue fear the wrath of the mob. For many decades in Arab countries, and among Palestinians, the mob has been a potent and formidable political force. In the past decade the Jewish mob has become a reality in Israel. Right-wing Jews frequently coalesce into an Arab-hating mob that has been a dangerous political force. As mentioned, when Israeli mobs recently conducted pogroms in Arab towns and in sections of Jerusalem, the police looked on placidly. As a political phenomenon the mob does not embrace any principles of justice. It craves a so-called strong leader. It instigates and sanctions violence as a way of life, and especially as a legitimate response to a hated adversary. Unfortunately, many of the pro-dialogue Israelis and Palestinians, and especially some of the political figures who are pro-dialogue, always seem to be partially listening to the immoral cries of the mob. They seem to be watching its screaming responses out of the corner of their eyes. This attitude is unfortunate; we believe it to be counterproductive. A worker for dialogue must confront the mob and forcefully reject its lack of principles, its embracing of violence as a way of life. But we did not want to edit such attitudes out of this book, and the reader may encounter authors watching the mob out of the corner of their eye.

Someone may suggest that probably it cannot be otherwise. The foundations of political freedom in the Middle East, where such freedom exists, are flimsy. In Israel, which is currently the country with the greatest political freedom, democracy was foisted from above. But this foisting did not include the drafting of a constitution and a bill of rights. Furthermore, today in Israel, four decades after independence, there is almost no grassroot democratic tradition; Jewish and Arab tribal attitudes quite often dominate the political scene. In Arab countries the lack of political freedom is much more evident. No Arab regime is currently democratic. Hence many spokespersons for freedom and dialogue must be wary. They dare not wander too far away from tribal consensus.

But if to understand a person's motives is to partially justify his or her deeds, we do not wish to understand or to justify unwillingness to confront the mob. Compromising dialogue so as to embrace tribal consensus is an abandoning of the courageous stance that dialogue demands. It is antidialogical.

Hold it, someone may say. In defining dialogue as a categorical imperative, in placing dialogue as a priority in your life, in believing that dialogue will bring about a major change, are you not dreaming? Perhaps. But we share this dream with some of the authors whose writings appear in the following chapters. Hence, if our dream of a just Israeli-Palestinian peace settlement is ever fulfilled, history may view this modest book as one of the first minor attempts to seek and to promote dialogue in an area of the world characterized by violence, political hostility, and interfaith antagonism for decades.

A second lesson has to do with what we call, for lack of a better term, cleanliness of discourse. Since Socrates attacked the rhetoric of sophists such as Gorgias and Protagoras, it is clear that genuine dialogue often requires that one speak without the mists of flourishing eloquence that has characterized rhetoricians for centuries. As mentioned above, in dialogue there is no attempt to manipulate the listener or the conversation. One addresses one's topic directly, without embroidering one's discourse, or leading one's listeners into verbal traps. (We know that Socrates did not always live up to this requirement. For instance, his arguments with Thrasymachus in the first book of *The Republic* are very manipulative. But Socrates did indicate the way.)

We explicitly requested from our authors that they make no attempts at manipulative rhetoric. We feel that they have succeeded. The result is that the discussions in the book are about principles of justice and of community, about the possibilities that genuine dialogue can bring forth, about one's personal experiences in struggling for dialogue, about confronting political evil, about the quest for integrity in a situation of oppression. Hence, the book has few traces of the bickering, the backstabbing, and the bitterness that have emerged in many discussions about the political future of this troubled area of the world. This cleanliness of discourse from manipulative elements greatly encouraged us as editors.

But as Socrates soon learned, cleanliness of discourse can be threatening. Many of his partners in dialogue preferred to live in the smog of unclean concepts and ideas that prevailed. Such is undoubtedly also true of the residents of Israel and the occupied territories. We know that the mere publication of this book will anger many extremists and religious fanatics among Israelis and Palestinians. These extremists feel that their hatred of others, their belligerent chauvinism, their dread of the good, are all threatened by the clean ideals and lucid ideas that the authors present.

A third lesson has to do with what Martin Buber called the ontic quest for dialogue, which he believed characterizes human existence. Our personal odyssey in putting together this book convinced us, once again, that even in a conflict-engulfed area, such as the Middle East, the ontic quest for dialogue, which Buber described as central to human existence, can emerge and can direct persons to seek after a more humane manner of relating to each other. To embrace such a dialogical attitude, to allow one's ontic quest for dialogue to emerge, one need not be a journalist, or a writer, or a lawyer, or a university professor, as are some of the authors who have participated in this book. Dialogue, Buber said, can emerge even in a fistfight. Here is a recent pertinent example.

The Israeli daily newspaper *Hadoshot* carried the following story about a Palestinian village near Nablus in which many youths had been active in the *intifada* by throwing rocks at Israeli army vehicles and hanging Palestinian flags on high. Usually the army would respond by chasing after the rock-throwing youths and beating them or wounding them with rubber bullets. The army would also immediately tear down and confiscate any Palestinian flag. One day a group of teenage youths in this village were playing soccer when they saw an Israeli army jeep approaching. Many of the youths ran for cover, but six or seven remained to see what would happen. The jeep stopped near the soccer field and five young soldiers got off. They approached the Palestinian youths and one of them said: "Hey, let's have a short soccer match." The Palestinian youths agreed but under one condition: whoever loses has to hoist and unfurl in the wind the flag of the winning team. They played for about twenty minutes and the Israelis lost. True to their word, the Israeli soldiers took a confiscated black, white, red, and green Palestinian flag out of the back of the jeep and fastened it to the jeep antenna. It waved in the wind for about ten minutes.

As the story indicates, mutual respect and dialogue can emerge even between adversaries such as the rock-throwing youths and the Israeli soldiers who are the major opponents in the *intifada*. The worker for dialogue can and should always be aware of what Buber called our ontic quest for dialogue. In everyday encounters, one should attempt to arouse that quest. As some of the authors in this book indicate, such is no easy task. Not only is one often faced with adamant responses, but also one's own fears, frustrations, and past personal sufferings often interfere.

A fourth lesson, which has already been intimated, should once again be emphasized. It has to do with the personal responsibility that emerges in the writings of the authors. The persons who speak out for dialogue in this book have taken upon themselves a grave, and at times a dangerous, responsibility, in addition to a daily struggle. In the Middle East, where violence and hostility between Palestinians and Israelis is a daily occurrence, where opening a newspaper means reading an account of yesterday's wounded and killed in this ongoing violence—in such an area, working for dialogue and speaking out for dialogue enrage the religious fanatics and the nationalistic elements of one's society. It can enrage the mob, or merely one's neighbors, who do not want to get involved in the fray. The sensitive reader will feel some such difficulties in the sections that follow.

Thus it is not an exaggeration to state that almost every one of the participants in this book, including the editors, has suffered for his or her views. Many of the Palestinians have been jailed or interrogated by Israelis or threatened by fellow Palestinians; many of the Israelis have been vehemently criticized, received hate mail, death threats, and some have been partially ostracized. Despite this suffering—and this is the point we want to make—one senses in the writings a personal responsibility for the difficult situation in which we Israelis and Palestinians find ourselves and a wish to find just means so as to change this situation. It is often this responsibility and this search for justice that has led the participants to engage in dialogue. In short, we believe that a great merit of the book is that it is not sterile. Fears and frustrations have seeped into many sentences. How could it be otherwise? Furthermore, most of the authors know that they have been marked by their ongoing struggle for Israeli-

Palestinian dialogue. The book often reeks of these authors' blood, sweat, and tears.

One interesting outcome of this personal involvement and difficult struggle is that although the authors in this book give varying definitions of dialogue, they are united in the belief that dialogue requires that they assume responsibility for changing the sad situation in which they find themselves. They grasp dialogue as an engagement, a confrontation, a way of life, not a social gathering, or mere negotiations or some sort of transaction. Furthermore, the authors sense that dialogue demands authenticity, transparency to oneself, honesty. It demands relating to others at eye level, as Zvi Gilat puts it in his article. All these make for a new responsible manner of relating to the difficulties that confront Jews and Arabs in the Middle East, which is both encouraging and refreshing.

We have divided the book into six sections. In each section an Israeli and a Palestinian who have been working for dialogue relate to a major topic that the worker for dialogue must face. Each section includes a short introduction, which presents the background of the participants and suggests how to read a bit between the lines. (Perhaps we should add that we are pleased that this book includes almost an equal number of men and women authors: seven women and six men. We feel that the broad participation of women in such a book is especially important for Israel and for the occupied territories, which are areas in which male chauvinism prevails.)

The first section, "Dialogue and Vision," with essays by Shulamit Aloni and Faisal Husseini, points out that dialogue between Palestinians and Israelis has a central role in helping one envision a peaceful, communal future for all the nations of the Middle East. Both authors stress that without such dialogue not only will violence, aggression, and hatred probably continue to reign in this region, but also many of the political, economic, social, and cultural achievements of the nations in this area — including the achievements of democratic Israel — are gravely endangered.

The second section, "Dialogue and Religious Life," with essays by Naim Ateek and Leah Shakdiel, suggests that the

Christian and Jewish heritage encourages dialogue with one's neighbors and fellow inhabitants of a country, and not the fanaticism that frequently emerges in this region. (Unfortunately, we did not find a Muslim contributor for this section.) We feel this section to be most important because of the prevalence of religious chauvinism, fanaticism, and fatalism in the Middle East. Of course, neither fanaticism nor fatalism nor chauvinism can live with the freedom and the mutual trust that emerge in moments of interfaith dialogue.

Since much of the oppression of Palestinians has to do with the draconian laws by which Israel rules the Palestinian people, we decided that the third section should include testimonies of an Israeli and a Palestinian lawyer. We should add that both Felicia Langer and Ziad Abu Zayad, who present their personal testimonies in this section, have had broad writing careers. Felicia Langer has written six books about her work as a Jewish lawyer defending the rights of Palestinians in Israeli courts. Ziad Abu Zayad has spent many years in journalism for the Palestinian press. Both lawyers, while relating dialogically, concentrate on principles of justice, and are willing to struggle for justice in their activities in the courts, and in their daily life. Their writing is often a crystalization of this struggle for justice and for dialogue.

We firmly believe that one can be educated for dialogue, hence the fourth section in which two educators, co-editor Haim Gordon and Hanan Mikhail-Ashrawi, dean of humanities at Birzeit University, present their views on the importance of dialogue, on the sad consequences of the failure of dialogue in the present situation, and how one must approach dialogue. But these essays should not suggest to the reader that they are typical of the academic scene in Israeli and Palestinian universities. Unfortunately, there are very few persons who express concern as to the lack of Israeli-Palestinian dialogue in the university milieu. Furthermore, persons who struggle for dialogue in this milieu, such as these writers do, are very rare. We can say straightforwardly that one of the telling signs of the difficult situation that confronts the worker for dialogue is that there are very few Israeli and Palestinian academics and educators who are deeply committed to Israeli-Palestinian dialogue.

The fifth section is dedicated to the struggle of two prominent Palestinian women, who have been diligently working for years for Israeli-Palestinian dialogue. But here is the catch. Mariam Mar'i is an Israeli citizen who resides in Acre, and Zahira Kamal is a resident of East Jerusalem, which means that she is a Palestinian without political rights and with few civil rights. Thus, Mariam Mar'i can attack Israel's oppressive policies against Palestinians from within, while Zahira Kamal must guard her statements, because an unguarded statement can land her in jail for inciting against the regime. The contrast between these women's political status emerges in their essays. In addition to this contrast, we believe this section is significant because it emphasizes the fact, not well enough known, that Palestinian women are in the foreground of the struggle for Palestinian-Israeli dialogue.

The final section of the book, with essays by Haidar Abdel Shafi and Zvi Gilat, reveals that Martin Buber was right when he stated categorically that dialogue is one of the bases for human integrity. Almost a generation and a half separate Haidar Abdel Shafi, a retired medical doctor born in Gaza at the end of World War I, and Zvi Gilat, an Israeli journalist in his thirties. Their respective styles of presenting their views reveal this generation gap. Yet their conclusions are very similar: human integrity can return to this troubled region of the world only through the mutual respect and trust that arise when persons engage in genuine dialogue.

In an area as volatile and as unstable as the Middle East, one can hardly suggest what the political situation will look like when this book reaches its readers. For instance, the international crisis evoked by Saddam Hussein's invasion of Kuwait was not envisioned by the authors when they wrote their essays. At this time we do not know how this crisis will be resolved and what influence it will have on the status of Israeli-Palestinian dialogue.

Despite the feeling in times of such crises that we seem to be sitting on a keg of gunpowder, we do hope and pray that dialogue between Israelis and Palestinians as equal partners will become a reality in the near future, and that Palestinians will soon live as a free people in their land alongside Israel. Unfortunately, we gravely doubt that this dream will soon be realized. But even if this dream is soon fulfilled, we believe that this book will still retain its important and humane message. Because it includes the live testimonies of a group of simple persons who courageously strive to end strife, hatred, and violence in the Middle East by means of mutual respect, a quest for justice, and genuine dialogue.

SECTION 1

DIALOGUE AND VISION

For many Israelis and Palestinians the everyday reality of conflict, oppression, and terrorism, which has characterized the relations between their peoples at least since Israel's occupation of the West Bank and the Gaza Strip, seems to leave no room for a vision of a better future. Residents of this area seem to have forgotten their own histories. Some of the most profound and resounding visions concerning humanity and communal life between nations were first spoken in this land, which is holy to the three monotheistic faiths. These resounding visions were uttered in difficult political circumstances, probably much more difficult than today's circumstances. The Hebrew prophets and Jesus dared to present their dreams of a better future, even when their lives were endangered by their fervent addresses and appeals. Today one cannot find more than a few persons who are willing to present even a simple vision of peace, dialogue, and communal living. Realpolitik, and with it indifference to justice, seem to have usurped all quests for true community.

When such an attitude prevails, those of us who do dream of dialogue and peace are often derided as naive, or even as stupid. To counter this trend we convinced two charismatic, down-to-earth, successful political leaders—both have had much experience of struggling against approaches based primarily on Realpolitik—to participate in this book, and to present their vision of dialogue and peace.

Shulamit Aloni is currently leader of the Civil Rights and

17

Peace party. She has been a member of the Israeli Knesset for more than twenty-five years, and has been struggling daily for human rights and civil rights during this quarter-century. Her vision of community in the Middle East is a component of this daily struggle. She forcefully rejects the cynicism of Realpolitik, even though she knows that she must live with the propounders of this approach in the Knesset. In short, again and again one realizes that she is a wonderful, refreshing phenomenon in Israeli politics, because she has not abandoned her spiritual roots and her faith in the victory of freedom while struggling daily in the political realm.

Faisal Husseini is a prominent leader of the Palestinians who live under Israeli rule, some would call him *the* prominent leader. Since he belongs to the famous Husseini family, which in the 1930s and 40s actively fought against Jewish settlement in Israel, he has been carefully watched by the Israel Security Service and has been jailed a number of times. Most recently, he spent six months incarcerated under the law of administrative detention, which means that no reason for his being jailed needs to be given. Despite this continual harassment and suffering, Husseini has become one of the most forceful speakers for Israeli-Palestinian dialogue in Israel-Palestine. His vision of a community of nations living peacefully on this land has both encouraged many workers for dialogue and enraged many Jewish and Arab fanatics.

Beyond their presenting a vivid vision of peace and community, Aloni and Husseini are united in an ontic quest. They both are willing to go beyond our Israeli-Palestinian mutual past of mistakes, sins, and crimes, of oppression and terrorism, and to speak out for a future of mutual respect and justice. That is where they transcend most of the political rhetoric that emerges from the Middle East. The lack of respect for human beings and their suffering, the lack of respect for their civil and political rights, is rampant in this area of the world. Justice is also not something that most residents of this area believe can be attained by political means. Historians will, of course, tell us that the reason for such lack of respect and for such a disregard of justice is that Islamic countries and the Jewish people in the diaspora never underwent the period of liberalism that has characterized the Western world. Even if this conclusion is correct, it does not mean that the disregard of justice, the disrespect for human suffering, and the oppression of civil and political rights must continue to reign unmolested.

Shulamit Aloni and Faisal Husseini firmly believe that if we follow the path of dialogue, if we strive for mutual respect and for justice, we can change our being-in-the-world. They offer us a simple vision of how that change would look, and some suggestions as to how dialogue may lead us to reach that destination.

1

The Quest for Human Rights and the Need for Dialogue: Two Sovereign Peoples

Shulamit Aloni

Quite often I feel as if I am climbing a down-going escalator. I have already climbed up many steps, but I remain in the same spot. For instance, in 1965, a quarter-century ago, when I was first asked by Prime Minister Levi Eshkol to join the Labor Party slate as a candidate for the Israeli Knesset, I set a few stiff conditions. Among them I wanted the Labor Party to modify its platform and to support the drafting of a constitution in Israel and especially a bill of rights. After some deliberation within the party, my conditions were met, and the platform was altered. After the elections the Labor Party continued to be in power, and there was even a beginning of work in the Knesset toward the drafting of a constitution. Yet today, twenty-five years later, Israel still lacks a constitution and a bill of rights. All this despite my continuous struggle in the Knesset, my continuous speaking out, and explaining about our dire need to formulate a constitution and to adopt a bill of rights.

Looking back, I believe that the year 1967 when, following the Six Day War, Israeli troops occupied the West Bank and the Sinai Peninsula—that year was the turning point. Before that many of us who cherished human freedom still believed that here in Israel we Jews were building a just society; we believed that we were moving toward a society whose principles would be in accordance with the United Nations universal declarations on human rights and their implied conventions, a society that would be willing to learn from the principles of freedom enunciated by the founding fathers of the United States and from the human rights formulated by the thinkers of the French Revolution. In the wake of the colonialist developments that followed the 1967 military victory, our beliefs began to erode. But not only our beliefs. The entire Israeli value system eroded. Parallel to this erosion there were decisions by the government and legislation passed by the Knesset that denied justice, freedom, and human rights to the Arabs living under Israeli military rule in the occupied territories. Put briefly, we began to create a political realm in which moral considerations are the concern of what in Hebrew we call "beautiful souls"—that is, persons with no down-to-earth understanding.

I mention all this because without respect for human rights and for the sovereign rights of our fellow human beings by Israeli leaders and by the people of Israel, there is little chance that we Israelis, as a nation, can initiate dialogue between Israelis and Palestinians. My years of parliamentary work have been very much dedicated to emphasizing the importance of human and civil rights. (At first I was called Mrs. Human Rights with derision, later with appreciation.) Hence I dismiss with ridicule all those Israeli politicians who say that they believe only in Realpolitik—that is, that there are no moral decisions within the political realm, only decisions of interest. These shallow politicians simply do not understand that moral decisions by definition are made under difficult circumstances, when interests are in conflict, not when everything is flowing smoothly.

Unfortunately I must say that since 1967 our manner of relating to Palestinians in the occupied territories has been immoral; it has been very much based on a philosophy of yours is mine and mine is mine. We have forcefully taken away their lands; we have degraded them by denying them basic human rights, civil rights, and political rights, and in the process we have violated many international laws and agreements. This deliberate policy of denying basic freedoms has influenced our own lives as a political community and as persons. For instance, we have even reached the ethnocentric stage whereby representatives of religious parties in Israel are not afraid to announce in the Knesset that anyone who struggles for human rights is attacking the holy religious sages of Judaism. Therefore, we must reject a bill of rights. Small wonder that dialogue with Palestinians is not on many Israelis' agenda.

Despite my many struggles for human and civil rights, I must admit that for years only few Israelis were sensitive to these issues. One major reason is that the founders of Israeli society never underwent the struggle for liberalism that occurred in Western Europe. Thus we have no liberal tradition in the Zionist movement, and in the period prior to the establishment of the state of Israel. Most of the Zionist leaders went from the backward society of Russia and Poland straight to the Marxist and other varieties of class socialism that developed in Israel. For instance, Ben Gurion did not accept the communist Leninist Weltanschauung. The society he attempted to build in Israel was Bolshevik in its demands that everything be approved from above, and in its creating a situation in which almost everyone was dependent on the party bureaucracy. If there was a minority that disagreed with the party line, he tried to co-opt it; and if he failed, he tried to exclude it from participation in political life. The party, the class, the nation, and *not* the individual were essential.

Furthermore, the same approach was adopted by the leaders of Jewish communities that came to Israel from the Mediterranean and Middle Eastern countries. In the diaspora and afterward in the prestate period in the land of Israel and in the Zionist movement, all organizations were voluntary; there was a recognition of political parties, and decisions were made by majority rule. I suspect that this may be one of the sources of the Israeli conception that democracy is essentially the existence of different parties and majority rule; in other words, a formal conception of democracy not based on communal values, without a unique status for the individual, and without tolerance of minorities. The sad result is that as a nation we have no understanding of the need for a political system based on checks and balances that help rein in the tyranny of the majority and ensure personal and political freedom. Put differently, Israel is a democracy without a liberal tradition.

I have not mentioned that the right-wing Likud Party under Menachem Begin has its sources in the Italian fascism of Mussolini and the nationalism of Pilsutzki of Poland, which stresses that we are first of all members of a nation whose needs predominate, with one flag, with a mutual belief in national myths. They also declare that we must all fight as one body for our nation's existence, and that our nation is allowed to take the promised land from its enemies by force. From here it is a short step to their hallowing of the entire land of Israel.

Add to all this that the tribal ethnocentric approach to Jewish existence in Israel, which determines by law each person's religious ethnic association, has also influenced our legislation, our judicial system, and our everyday nonliberal way of life. The case of the Jewish murderer Wiliam Nakash, who killed an Arab in France and then fled to Israel, is a case in point. Influenced by the religious parties, the minister of justice rejected France's demands that he be extradited, even though Nakash killed the Arab as a result of a war between drug peddlers on territory for peddling their drugs. Ratz, the political party that I represent in the Knesset, appealed the minister's decision to the high court of justice, and won. We stressed that the fact that Nakash had murdered an Arab made him no less a murderer.

Thus Israel's history has developed under the influence of a practical leftist Bolshevism countered by a right-wing myth-loving nationalism, both of which stifle all liberalism. Add to that the tribal approach of Orthodox Jews, and it is no wonder that the quest for human rights and the education for Jewish-Arab dialogue have been arduous, and quite often unsuccessful, undertakings.

Nevertheless, in my quest for human rights and dialogue I do not feel lonely. When I know that I am speaking out in the name of universally accepted principles, such as enunciated in the United Nations Charter, or in the Declaration on the Rights of Man, I never feel that I am alone. Moreover, there are now in

Israel quite a few people who have studied at universities, and they at least know what I am talking about when I mention human and civil rights. Unfortunately, at the secondary school level there is little education for appreciation of human rights, while there is much study of the status of Jews and their rights during our long history. Therefore, I am not surprised that our army deals brutally with the Palestinian uprising.

One aspect of our self-centeredness is that over the years we have made the Holocaust into an obsession that allows us Jews, the victims of this horrible history, to believe that—since we were victims—we can never do wrong. Instead of learning from the terrifying aspects of the Holocaust that we must embrace and pursue a broad humanism, we have used our sad history to develop a national egocentricism that allows, and often encourages, deep hatred of others to flourish. With this kind of a mood dominating our life, all the right-wing politicians need to do is to call Yasir Arafat a Nazi and thus encourage people to believe that all avenues of dialogue with him must be blocked.

Our staunch belief in our being the permanent victims of history has made even leading politicians blind to the destructiveness of their policies. Already in 1969 I spoke in the Knesset and said that we should not call the occupied territories "liberated territories," because there are people living there who hardly feel free of our military presence and they view us as conquerors. After I said these words Golda Meir, the prime minister, arose and yelled at me: "How dare you call Jews conquerors? Jews never were conquerors, are not conquerors, and never will be conquerors!" I suspect that she firmly believed that the Jewish army had full right to capture Palestinian land by force, to rule it, and under guidance of a Jewish government to do anything that government decided to the indigenous Palestinian population, and still Jews should not be called conquerors. It seems that in Golda's distorted thinking we were still the suffering victims.

A deep anxiety as to the future very often accompanies me. Not because of my failures to educate and to legislate for human rights and against Jewish tribalism. No. My main anxiety is from my realization that no matter how many steps I will ascend, no matter how many successes I will have in my struggle for human rights, the political escalator in which we now live is continuously moving down—I remain in the same spot. And this spot is my home, my society, it is my life's work, it encompasses the vistas of nature that I cherish, it is my entire life. And all my struggles to better this world are undercut by narrow and shallow political decisions, which are influenced by supercilious, fundamentalist religious and nationalist approaches.

I firmly believe that our relations with the Palestinians can now be solved by simple rational discussion. Whether we like it or not, there are two political entities in the land of Israel-Palestine. One entity, Israel proper, lies within the green line that was agreed upon in the armistice agreement of 1949. And the other entity includes the geographical territories inhabited by the Palestinian people on the West Bank and in the Gaza Strip. Israel proper is a state with the instruments for democratic rule: a Knesset, a judicial system, a seemingly free press, and so forth. The Palestinians in their own country are ruled by the Israeli military using military laws and means. They have almost no civil rights and no political rights. If we accept the United Nations decision that the age of imperialism has passed from the world, we have no business sitting in the country of the Palestinians, exploiting them, and oppressing them by military means.

Furthermore, like Hegel's "master-slave relationship," we are enslaved by our acts of oppressing the freedom of others. We masters will have no freedom as long as we continue to deny freedom to the Palestinians. For years we argued that we cannot speak with the Palestinians because they do not recognize the existence of Israel and reject U.N. resolutions 242 and 338. Now the Palestinian National Council has recognized Israel and accepted these resolutions. They rescinded the use of terror. Now is the time to sit down and in a spirit of dialogue discuss how to establish a viable peace in the area in which the security of Israel will be ensured. In the process of this discussion our military forces will retreat from the West Bank and the Gaza Strip, and the Palestinians will establish their own state.

I believe that such a step can lead to peace with all our Arab neighbors and to economic growth. In the Casablanca meeting of the Arab league the decisions of the Palestinian National Council were approved. This means acceptance of U.N. General Assembly decision 181 of November 29, 1947, which partitions the area of the British Mandate of Palestine between two nations. It also includes U.N. Security Council decisions 242 and 338, which ensure Israel's secure existence in its area. Therefore our politicians are not speaking truthfully when they say that accepting a Palestinian state will lead to war with the other Arab states. They are misleading their listeners, because we have had peace with Egypt for more than a decade, we have a de facto peace with Jordan, and we have had a cease-fire with Syria since 1974, which the Syrians have kept despite our uncalled for provocations in Lebanon. Of course there are differences, but I am sure they can be settled by negotiations and dialogue.

In this hopeful scenario, what I fear most are the fundamentalists — the Jewish fundamentalists as much as the Muslim fundamentalists. The basic problem of these fundamentalists is that they do not respect the religious beliefs and the holy places of their neighbors. They want it all for themselves. For instance, those Jews who want to build a new temple on the Temple Mount, on that piece of land where two famous Muslim mosques have stood for centuries, are acting with total disrespect for their Muslim neighbors. In addition they are lighting the fuse of a religious war, which could end in a jihad or a war of mutual destruction. Hence, fundamentalism is the greatest enemy of those of us, Jews and Arabs, who believe in mutual respect and dialogue.

I have spent quite a bit of time lately traveling to international forums set up to foster Israeli-Palestinian dialogue. I felt that these meetings are a manner of slowly legitimizing the possibility of Israeli-Palestinian dialogue — a possibility that our current government rejects. At these dialogues we are breaking an Israeli taboo, and by involving more and more people in such international meetings we are showing that this breaking of the taboo can lead to a new conception of our life here in the Middle East.

At these forums I tell my Palestinian counterparts that our people need time to adjust to the idea that the Palestinian Liberation Organization (PLO), after forty years of enmity, recognizes the right of Israel to exist and is willing to renounce terror and its claim to the entire land, a claim that appears in the Palestinian Covenant. I tell them that they should continue to emphasize their willingness to live as our neighbors and to negotiate with us in dialogue. Only a constant emphasizing of this theme will convince the Israelis to sit down and talk to them. I do not tell them how they must run their country or their liberation movement. Of course, I will express my rejection of terror, my fears of fundamentalists of all stripes; I will also tell them that I abhor murder and war; but I will not be paternalistic to them in any way. Dialogue is between equals and I relate to them as my equals. They are representatives of the Palestinians just as I am a representative of the Israelis. But my main arguments are directed to the Israeli government. This government must sit with the Palestinians and with the PLO now, and talk about peace.

The time has come for the Israeli government and the people of Israel to understand that the Israeli government has no right to cause daily bloodshed in the occupied territories, to enlist its young people in the army for three to five years, to call up reserves for extended periods—an act that gravely hurts the economy and the quality of life in Israel—and in addition to inflict brutal, unjust suffering upon Palestinians while denying them human and civil rights. These policies are pursued in the name of a nationalistic ideology and supported by religious myths.

The continuing of the current occupation of the West Bank and the Gaza Strip is not done for security reasons, but rather to satisfy Jewish irredentist and colonialist desires. For the good of Israel and of the Jewish people in the world, and in order to establish a just society, based on a balanced economy, here in Israel, we must immediately establish an honest dialogue with the Palestinian people. We must make peace with them knowing that this land, Israel-Palestine, belongs to two nations, hence by definition both nations have rights for self-definition, for sovereignty, and for a life of freedom.

2

The Prospects of Dialogue: Accepting the PLO

Faisal Husseini

Perhaps the saddest aspect of Israel's current government leaders' adamant stance against dialogue with the recognized leaders of the Palestinian people is that this stance lacks vision. These leaders of Israel seem to respond to the past, they do not seem to be able to hope or to work for a better future; hence they suggest no new ideas on how to live peacefully in this region of the world. One of the things I have learned by observing developments in the European community and most recently in Eastern Europe is that small nations will thrive only if they live in peace and are able to create common markets and loosen border restrictions. Only thus will they be able to provide their inhabitants with an enhanced cultural and economic life.

The Middle East, including Israel, should begin to think in terms of increased international dialogue, which will lead to the establishment of a common economic market and a community of nations. If we do not want to lag behind in the twenty-first century, we must learn to live in dialogue at all levels—the personal level, the regional level, the international level. We Palestinians know enough about being excluded, due to our sad history during the past four decades.

The loss of Palestine in 1948 was a trauma of national dimensions. We lost not only much of our land and many of our villages and cities; more importantly, we also lost our social pyramid. Many Palestinians living in villages, towns, and cities in Palestine became refugees dispersed in camps and towns in various countries of the Middle East. Part of the Palestinian people was living in Israel, another part in the Gaza Strip under Egyptian administration, other Palestinians lived in Jordan under the Hashemite monarchy, and still others in Lebanon. If one could have formerly characterized our society as a pyramid, as a result of our people's dispersion this pyramid began to fall apart. But the Palestinian leadership that emerged following our defeat did not grasp this development. It continued to lead the Palestinian people on the basis of a political pyramid as a parallel to a social pyramid, which had in fact collapsed. Consequently, within two years the Palestinian people turned its backs on its old leadership and thus started an era in our history in which we were dispossessed of our land and bereft of leadership. The Palestinian people did not oppose that leadership, nor did they challenge it. It had simply become anachronistic.

This problem of our political leadership is significant because it explains the fragmentation of the political struggles, despite our common objectives. Put simply, the two stated goals of all the Palestinian people are the establishment of an independent state in our homeland and a coming together of the Palestinian people in that homeland. Despite agreement on these two goals, the struggle to attain them has not been done under one leadership, due to the objective conditions of the Palestinian people dispersed in the region. Consequently, the external conditions of dispossession and exile reflected themselves internally on the structure of Palestinian society and the unity and representative capacity of its leadership. Even the PLO, established in 1964, initially reflected the will of its patron Arab regimes instead of the unified collective will of the Palestinian people.

This situation began to change in 1967, after Israel occupied the West Bank and the Gaza Strip. Suddenly, Palestinians in the Gaza Strip could enter into dialogue with Palestinians in Israel and on the West Bank. Furthermore, because of the collapse of the iron fist of the Arab regimes in their own borders following the 1967 war, Palestinians from Lebanon, Syria, and Jordan moved freely in the area for several months, including crossing the Jordan River and communicating with Palestinians residing in the homeland. I remember that I traveled from Beirut to Damascus to Amman and then to Jerusalem and to the Gaza Strip without facing difficult obstacles. The inter-Palestinian dialogue that emerged during this period helped establish a new leadership that could control the PLO; thus the PLO became a Palestinian organization instead of an Arab organization set up for Palestinians. In other words through such dialogues the Palestinian people sensed the opportunity to reconstruct a new and legitimate Palestinian framework representing all Palestinians.

This reconstruction was accompanied by our continual struggle to attain an independent state and to end the Israeli occupation of our land. Israel rejected these aspirations and refused to consider our legitimate claims. Worse, the Israeli leadership refused to enter into dialogue with us; they viewed us as unwanted native inhabitants of a land they had captured and upon which their so-called pioneers had decided to settle. They did not, in fact, regard us as a people with national rights. On the other hand the struggle strengthened us as a people and deepened our relationship to our own leaders—we began to act as a people under one leadership.

For a variety of reasons, including the fact that we are a relatively small people and have no forests or high mountains in our country, the Israelis succeeded in pushing outside the country the main forces and organizations fighting for our freedom. Consequently, a series of complications and factors entered the Palestinian political and human equation that thrust us into the midst of conflicts beyond our will and scope. In addition to our internal contradictions and the conflict with the Israeli occupation, we had to face contradictions within our host countries and their people; we became inadvertently involved in their internal conflict. Thus began a period of complications and conflicts, which, against our will, forced us to fight battles not of our own making. The PLO, then, had to make decisions and take positions based on the external balance of strategic forces, and not primarily or necessarily reflecting Palestinian internal realities and interests. At the same time the Palestinians under occupation understood that they must remain steadfast, attached to the land. However, they always looked outside to the PLO as the source of hope and salvation. A division of tasks evolved, allocating steadfastness to the occupied and the struggle for liberation to the exiled.

Under occupation, the Palestinians took a passive role while relegating to the PLO the full weight of the struggle outside, and as spectators we analyzed, criticized, questioned, or approved their actions. We imposed on them the Herculean task of dealing with their impossible conditions surrounded by external pressures and forces, while holding them responsible for liberating us. It was during this stage that the long process of mobilization and organization was started by the PLO within the occupied territories in preparation for consolidating a popular base for the totality of the struggle.

The tremendous impact of the blow received by the PLO as a result of the Israeli invasion of Lebanon in 1982, and the subsequent removal of the PLO from the close vicinity of the occupied territories, formed the basic drive that led the Palestinians under occupation to take matters into their own hands and assume responsibilities that they had earlier relegated to the PLO. This, among others, formed a major motivation for the *intifada*. With the *intifada*, the massive popular Palestinian uprising, came a radical change of circumstances. Our struggle became normal. The Palestinian people began to struggle for political freedom on their land of Palestine. This struggle helped resolve many inner contradictions in our being and helped us confront the cruel and oppressive daily reality of Israeli occupation. Most important, the relationship between the Palestinians under occupation and the PLO became one of genuine representation. As genuine leadership, the PLO now enjoys the support and the legitimacy of its natural popular base—the whole Palestinian people. This favorable development was also a major cause in promoting the peace initiative that emerged from the nineteenth Palestinian National Council.

We Palestinians consider the PLO the embodiment of our struggle and our hope for our freedom and rights. We view with satisfaction the slow but finally successful struggle of the PLO to attain a political presence in the world, even after the difficult defeat in Lebanon and the lack of assistance of Arab countries. We view with pride its developing as a political body, which culminated in the call for dialogue with Israel in the discussions of the representatives of the Palestinian people at the meetings of the Eighteenth and Nineteenth Palestinian National Councils. We see in these developments steps toward our attaining freedom in our land and our regaining our dignity as a people. Thanks to these developments Palestinians throughout the world and hundreds of prominent statesmen in many countries and scores of states recognize the PLO as our legitimate representatives.

Personally, I have been active for freedom of our people and for dialogue with Israelis for many years. Born in Iraq in 1940, I was raised in Cairo where I joined the Palestinian Student League in 1959. In 1964 I joined the PLO office in Jerusalem, just after it opened. Although I attended officer's school in Damascus and Aleppo, in 1967 after the Israeli occupation I returned to Jerusalem where I continued to struggle, primarily by political means, for the freedom of the Palestinian people. Lately, some of our people hold that I have emerged as one of the leaders of the Palestinians in the West Bank and Gaza. But I suspect that people mainly started knowing me through my establishing of the Arab Studies Society in 1980, which is dedicated to research on Palestinian history, the development of Palestinian culture, and the furthering of Palestinian education. This important Palestinian institution has unfortunately been closed for two years by order of the Israeli authorities. Before that I was not a prominent figure in Palestinian activities. I should add though that the fact that I carry a Jerusalem identity card does not allow the Israeli authorities to deport me. I have taken advantage of this situation and have not hesitated to speak out forcefully for our rights. So for certain periods my name was probably more in the news than the names of others. Perhaps the fact that I have been jailed four times by the Israelis and have lived in town arrest for five years also led our people to learn more about me.

My experience as a political prisoner and the extremely harsh and painful conditions of my imprisonment have been shared by many Palestinians. Some suffered cruel treatment and torture. Nevertheless we remain committed to the peace process. To me this is a true measure of our commitment to dialogue and a genuine proof of the Palestinians' ability to transcend the present pain and oppression, and to project a future of vision and peace. In addition, dialogue, in spite of the oppression of the occupation, is a serious means of exposing the brutality and injustice of our conditions while striving to create an alternative peaceful reality based on equality and freedom.

I do not want to present in detail our sad history of occupation, of personal suffering, of oppression, and of Israeli-Palestinian violence. What is more important is to sit down and to talk, to conduct dialogue with one's enemy in order to start building the grounds for a better and more peaceful future. I would like to state clearly and unequivocally: we are not trying to destroy our enemy; all we want is to reach an agreement with it. We want to try to change the state of enmity to a situation of peaceful neighborly accommodation. In short, we want to reach peace with this enemy, to have dialogue with the visible representative of that enemy. We believe that such dialogue is the first significant step toward peaceful coexistence.

It is pointless for us to say what we think of Mr. Shamir, Mr. Peres, or of any Israeli leader. Is he an advocate of peace or of war? Is he speaking truthfully when he says that he wants peace? Is Mr. Shamir merely a terrorist, as he was in 1948? All these questions are irrelevant when one enters into dialogue in order to create a situation in which we may live peacefully as neighbors. Hence the question facing Israeli leaders and the people of Israel is: Do they want to liquidate their Palestinian enemy or to reach a solution with the Palestinians? If they want to reach a solution, this can be attained only by speaking with our representatives, that is with the PLO, and, at its head, Mr. Yasir Arafat. Again it is irrelevant what the Israelis think of the PLO and of Mr. Arafat. It is irrelevant if they view him as a terrorist or as an adventurer or as an advocate of peace. He is the man who represents the leadership of the Palestinians, and sooner or later they will have to speak with him if they want to reach peace.

And there is one more point to make here. For dialogue to succeed, it must occur between free, equal people. Thus if the Israelis tell us to stop the *intifada* and then they will speak with us or open the schools, or release some prisoners, they are not speaking to us as persons who are free and who are equal to themselves. The *intifada* should not be hostage to dialogue. Rather, it is a natural reaction to the occupation, and will stop only when the occupation no longer exists. Until such occurs the *intifada* will continue, because it is a movement of the Palestinian people toward building the authentic infrastructure of the Palestinian state. More. The *intifada* is a new morality, a new state of mind—the state of mind of a people who are willing to struggle for their freedom and who are actively building their future.

One of the significant developments that has forcefully emerged in the past few years is that a solution to the Palestinian problem is central and crucial for a comprehensive peace in the entire Middle East. And this solution must be based on the basic rights, aspirations, and wishes of the Palestinian people. It cannot be an externally imposed solution. We Palestinians see this development not only as a problem, but also as an opportunity— with the establishment of the Palestinian state, with the return of our people to their land, with our attaining of political freedom and national rights we believe that significant steps can be made to establish peace among all the peoples and nations of this area. This may sound like a dream, but I am stating it as a realist.

Let me give two examples to support this dream. If four years ago anyone would have proposed that the Palestinian people in the occupied territories rise up and with only stones in their hands create an independent political entity, the author of such a proposal would have been dismissed with derision. But these last three years have shown that without Phantom planes or Mercava tanks or other sophisticated up-to-date weapons, such has happened. Furthermore, we Palestinians have learned much during this period of open, forceful, and successful rebellion against the Israel defense force, which is one of the strongest armies in the area. We have learned to confront the brutal occupation and its ever-escalating repression with a brave and collective rejection of the methods of suppressing us. We have learned the necessity and the methods of disengaging ourselves from the network of the institutions set up by Israel as part of their manner of oppression, and to establish our alternative viable institutions. We have taken the initiative and expressed the genuine collective will of the Palestinians, independent of any external pressures or interests in the region. Most important, we have learned to see our day-to-day reality without confusing it with our dream, even while we strive to realize that just and legitimate dream.

The same is true of the acceptance of the principle of partition based on U.N. resolution 181 and of U.N. resolutions 242 and 338 (in conjunction with the right to self-determination) by the Palestinian National Council, and Mr. Arafat's denunciation of all forms of terror. A few years ago no one would have foreseen that the PLO would adopt these resolutions and agree to establishing a Palestinian state alongside Israel. But through a gradual process of discussion, analysis, and self-education, especially by the pragmatists who believed in a future based on dialogue with Israel, this decision was finally accepted by a large majority of the Palestinian people and adopted by our representatives in the Palestinian National Council.

I realize that many Israelis fear that the Palestinian proposal is only a tactical step, that it is only a stage, and that our real goal is to take over all of Palestine. I can only answer honestly that this is a dream that some Palestinians have, just as some Jews have a dream of evacuating all the Palestinians from what they call greater Israel. We both have a right to such dreams, but as I have told the Israelis more than once, if we want peace we must both leave aside such dreams, because what may seem a beautiful dream to one nation is a nightmare to its neighboring nation. And if we try to realize such nightmares, we will not engage in dialogue and not move toward peace. Also, we must put aside all the terrible nightmares that stem from fears of the other side. As a Palestinian I must put aside the terrible massacres of Palestinians in Dir Yasin and Kafr Kasem, and the

Israelis must put aside fears that stem from memories of the massacre at Hebron. We must leave aside all this kind of dreaming and start talking about how we can coexist peacefully here in the land where both our nations reside.

In short, the advocates of dialogue among the Palestinian people and leadership have convinced the majority of our people that the main goal of our struggle is to be free and not to enslave or to destroy other nations. We now believe that our major struggle is to create a state, a recognized political entity for our people, and not to demolish the state of our neighbor. We also believe that we are now struggling to ensure that future generations of all nations in the Middle East can live in freedom and security, and can pursue their life with dignity—and that includes the future generations of our present enemies. Again and again we have described these goals of our struggle to the Israelis, but their current government refuses to listen, refuses to become a partner to our suggested dialogue.

In addition to refusing to listen to our statements, the Israelis have not learned from the nonmilitary methods we are using during our struggle. By using such low-level violence in our struggle, by rejecting firearms as a means for attaining our freedom, we have been sending a clear message to the Israelis. We are struggling to liberate our own people, not to enslave another people; we are striving to establish our own state, not to destroy the state of others; we are fighting to ensure a secure future for our children, not to threaten the future generations of another people. Despite our declarations and manners of rejecting Israeli oppression, many Israelis still do not understand the real message of the *intifada* and the significance of the Palestinian peace initiative. Many still view us on the basis of stereotypes and prejudices. That is a major reason we decided in the third year of the *intifada* to try to engage in dialogue with as many Israelis as possible. We want to convince them to deal with facts and not with misconceptions, and to show them that dialogue with the Palestinian people is a viable alternative to the brutal and mutually destructive situation of occupation.

Hence, I can only close this short piece with a renewed call to all Israelis, but especially to Israeli leaders, to speak to the

PLO, to listen to the PLO, to deal with the PLO, and to negotiate with the PLO. Do not ignore the strong, clear voices for
dialogue that are calling out from among the Palestinian leadership and people.

SECTION 2

DIALOGUE AND RELIGIOUS LIFE

While the quest for interfaith dialogue has become acceptable in many Western countries and has often been promoted by
religious establishments and communities in those countries, in
the Middle East, the cradle of the three monotheistic faiths,
derision, hatred, and hostility between the faiths continue to
thrive. The ongoing brutal religious war in Lebanon and the
continual oppression of the Christian Copts in Islamic Egypt are
examples of this state of affairs. Thus it is no wonder that interfaith dialogue in Israel and Palestine is scarce. This scarcity
reflects the sad fact that among many believers in the Middle
East there is very little respect for adherents of another faith
and almost no interest in understanding the existential message
of that faith. There is almost no reaching out to believers of
other religions. In such a situation dogmatism reigns, smothering
the freedom that is the basis of each faith and not allowing the
fruits of freedom to emerge. Put differently, struggling for freedom in the Middle East usually has nothing to do with a life of
faith. Thus, what is currently called the resurgence of Islam, a
phenomenon that gained momentum with the rise of Ayatollah
Khomeini, is almost always totally divorced from a quest for
freedom—in many instances this resurgence is merely a manner
of renewed enslavement. Such a divorcing of faith from freedom

is also true for almost all of Orthodox Judaism in Israel and for some Christian sects.

Since we believe these dogmatic and fanatic trends to be betrayals of some of the deeper humane messages that are at the core of each monotheistic faith, we spent much effort in enlisting workers for dialogue from each faith who would show how their own quest for dialogue concurs with their religious beliefs. Despite our ongoing efforts, we failed in our attempts to find such a Muslim writer.

Naim Stifan Ateek is canon of St. George's Cathedral in Jerusalem and pastor of its Arabic-speaking congregation. Born in 1937 in Beth Shean, he and his family were forcefully evicted from their home in 1948 by the Israeli army and transferred to Nazareth. Despite this and other difficult experiences under Israeli rule, despite his deep awareness of the tragedy of the Palestinian people, Ateek is not bitter. He is a diligent worker for interfaith dialogue and a struggler for justice. He has published his thoughts on his pursuit of justice in his book *Justice, and Only Justice: A Palestinian Theology of Liberation* (Orbis Books). In his following essay he relies on his religious faith and his personal experience to explain how dialogue can and should lead to justice.

Leah Shakdiel is an Orthodox Jew and a feminist. She recently won a battle in the Israel Supreme Court against her fellow Orthodox Jews who wished to bar her from participating in the local religious council because such involvement did not fit a woman. After the court decision, she served on the religious council. She has been active in many dialogical meetings with Palestinians. In these discussions, as in the following essay, she often brought her religious background to the fore as a source of her quest for dialogue.

Shakdiel and Ateek are united in their staunch belief that their commitment to their own faith and religious heritage is a commitment to pursue justice and to strive for interfaith dialogue. They read the sacred texts as demanding a moral and humane response to the terrible situation of oppression and terrorism in which Israelis and Palestinians find themselves. They seek ways of interpreting these texts that will allow Israelis and Palestinians, Jews and Christians, to live together in peace.

They forcefully reject dogmatism and a faith that allows enslavement of other human beings.

Perhaps we should say it again. Such an approach to one's faith is rare, very rare in this troubled area of the world. Hence, the writings of Naim Stifan Ateek and Leah Shakdiel are like a cool breeze after a dusty *khamsin*. They are also a worthy challenge to their fellow believers.

3

Dialogue as an Opportunity for Spiritual Growth: Linking Tradition with Creativity

LEAH SHAKDIEL

In the collective memory of the Jewish people, dialogues with non-Jews cause apprehension and a feeling of threat: anti-Semitic Christians time and again imposed on rabbis theological contests, deliberately staged to humiliate Jews and to justify their inferior political status. Jewish leaders usually prepared for the task as for martyrdom, and when they managed to hold their ground throughout such trials, gained the halo of national heroes. I think that this is how Jews understood the late Yaakov Herzog, Israeli ambassador to Canada, when he dared to counter with an eloquent essay Arnold Toynbee's statement that the Jewish people is more of a fossil than a living nation. In a sense, many Jews expect all Israeli diplomats and politicians to do the same — to present to the world the case of a proud and distinctive people no longer willing to remain an underdog. In short, what many Jews have in mind is a soliloquy, not a real dialogue, which requires reciprocity.

I propose that when we approach dialogue with present-day Palestinians we do not draw upon precedents from the painful and complicated history of relationships between Jews and non-

Jews. We should instead look toward other instances of mutual exchange in our tradition. Two examples come to mind.

There is a Chasidic story about a rabbi who used to spend a very long time with every person who came to see him. When asked what took him so long, he said: "Every time the other person speaks, I must take off my clothes and put his on, as it is written in the Mishna, 'Do not judge your friend until you are in his place.' And then when it is my turn to speak or give advice, I must take off his clothes and put mine back on." A meaningful meeting, then, should combine the two seeming opposites — empathy with the other and assertion of one's own identity.

One of my favorite quotes from medieval biblical commentaries is Rashbam's account of a dispute he had with his grandfather Rashi, the most renowned commentator of all ages. In the end the old man admitted that if he had had the strength, he would have written a new interpretation of the Torah, "due to insights that get renewed every day." From this short vignette I learn that a fruitful dialogue can exist not only between contemporaries but also between people of different generations, between a self and its own past insights, between a self and a changing world, and that all of this happens simultaneously.

From my experience, dialogue works only if both parties know that it involves exposing one's own weaknesses, as well as revealing unpleasant truths about the other; and only if both parties know that the experience will change them. Dialogue means spelling out conflicts, including perhaps implied and unconscious ones, toward a resolution that is never an act of simple addition or subtraction, but rather a new creation. I come to the dialogues in which I participate as an artist prepared for a trying group exercise designed to free a block in my creativity, yet confident that my autonomous being will survive the experience, precisely because I will be able to embrace the new vision as my better self.

It remains to apply all of this to a new historical reality: a dialogue between Israeli Jews and Palestinians. But first a bit about my background.

I am an Orthodox Jew. Many people stereotype secular thinking as open-minded and religion as reactionary and resistant to change. In my experience, dogmatism, or the tendency to fossilize opinions and positions, cuts across the board.

I was raised in a modern religious educational system that contained a built-in contradiction. On the one hand, it inculcated in us humility in the presence of the Almighty, who gave us humans one unchangeable book of laws and has empowered prophets, and then rabbis, with a fairly limited albeit exclusive mandate to interpret the laws for us in every generation. Breaking the law is not just a sin that brings personal punishment; it is an act of treason. One might say that every Jewish sinner drills a hole in the boat of Jewish history and threatens to drown the entire Jewish people. On the other hand, religious studies in our school took the form of a journey through layers of rabbinical interpretations and unfolded for us an exciting and courageous drama of incessant dynamism, creative responses to forever changing circumstances, and inevitable controversies.

I now believe that nothing could prepare me better for a life in a world of ambiguities, where the real moral task is often to balance such conflicts as the divine and the earthly, principle and circumstance, vision and reality, nationalism and universalism, tradition and progress, communal responsibility and personal autonomy. Idolatry, we learned, is an attempt to·interpret the world as a collection of frozen, immobile forces. Judaism set out to shatter all idols in the name of the one living God, who commands humankind to struggle for universal peace and justice. We Jews, we were told, are the one nation chosen for this godly task, and the vehicle is divine law, *halakah* in Hebrew, from the root "go" — always on the move, always changing, even if the changes are tiny and perceptible only to those with sound training in talmudic dialectic. The ignorant world claims that *halakah* is solid matter; we the initiated experience daily the simmering of its molecules.

In short, Jewish religion for me is a liberating rather than an oppressive force, a dialogue between differences rather than a monolithic discipline. I am sure that in our need to give birth to a new reality of peace in this part of the world, we can draw upon this source.

My parents, by adopting Zionism, quarreled openly with their own parents, broke away from the rich texture of Polish Jewry, and emigrated to Palestine where harsh conditions prevailed. Those who stayed behind were murdered by the Nazis, but we, the survivors, were taught to feel lucky, not self-righteous.

My grandparents, like many religious Jews at that time, based their opposition to Zionism on the following passage from the Babylonian Talmud, a text that had kept the lid on national longings for many centuries:

> One should always reside in the Land of Israel, even in a town which is populated by a majority of idolators, but one should not reside outside the Land of Israel, even in a town which has a majority of Jews; since everyone who resides in the Land of Israel is like one who has a God, and everyone who resides outside the Land of Israel is like one who has no God, as it is said (Lev. 25:28): "To give you the land of Canaan to be your God."
>
> These three oaths—what for? One, that [the people of] Israel shall not come up against the wall. And one, that the holy One, blessed be He, made [the people of] Israel swear that they will not rebel against the nations of the world. And one, that the holy One, blessed be He, made the idolators swear that they will not oppress [the people of] Israel too much.

This talmudic interpretation of history became binding law for many Jews. It stipulates that we are forbidden by holy oath to struggle for our national independence, and must wait for the messiah to deliver us from exile and reestablish Jewish sovereignty in our land. In the meantime, we cherish life on the land as individuals, a religious value that goes well with the predominant Muslim tolerance of "the People of the Book."

What impressed me most about the dramatic turnabout in religious discourse undertaken by people like my parents was the urge to transcend the circumstances of their birth, to plunge into an unknown future, to commit themselves to the realization of a utopian vision by claiming that it was indeed nourished by the accumulated energy of generations of frustrated faith in Zion. They rebelled against what they saw as spiritual stagnation, claimed they were only liberating a potential within tradition itself, and never stopped searching for bridges between Zionism and the Torah world. The simmering of the molecules was precipitated to the point of boiling, but for them remaining connected to Jewish tradition was valued above all. I am committed to another spiritual transformation now—of religious thinking, social patterns, political frameworks—from chauvinism and militarism to peace and justice; but, like my parents, I believe it can succeed only if we keep alive the dialogue with our past, with our many selves imbedded in our sources.

What I treasure in my dialogues with Palestinians are moments when they tell me about their past, their national history, the changes in their consciousness, their myths and traditions, including those they reject. I cried when I heard Dr. Nabil Shaat, Yasir Arafat's political emissary, quote a biblical story to emphasize the shift in the PLO toward the two-state solution: the Palestinians, he said, were like the mother who told King Solomon to give her baby to the other woman to avoid cutting him in half, but now they understand that a land, unlike a baby, can be divided.

The story was a perfect choice for the occasion—the groundbreaking, heavily televised Road to Peace Conference, in New York, in March 1989. But similar testimonies of change and reinterpretation are shared in private conversations, as well as in carefully staged group discussions to which I am invited occasionally. Thus, in June 1987, before the *intifada* and the PLO acceptance of U.N. resolutions 242 and 338 (which implies de facto recognition of the state of Israel), when dialogue was still a dangerous activity that had to be concealed, I felt shaken when Dr. Rhada Tallahami, a Palestinian political scientist who lives in Chicago, reached out to comfort us with her own tears when news of a murder of a Jewish boy by terrorists almost tore apart a well-meaning and courageous meeting orchestrated by Professor Herb Kellman in Radcliffe. It was important to hear her denounce the act, to hear about controversy inside the PLO, about an inner movement toward change—because we, the Jewish counterparts, had to impart our own disagreement with our government and tell about our efforts toward change.

When I visited Mary Khass, a social worker from Haifa who

gave up her Israeli citizenship in order to live and work in Gaza, I could relate to the familiar clues in her talk: "these bastards" [fanatical Moslem terrorists], "these bourgeois males, I have no patience for them" [Gaza notables, politicians of different factions], "I can't sleep, what do I say to the child who hid under the bed when the soldiers burst in at midnight and dragged his father away" [the frustrating helplessness of civil rights workers]? I recognize in her activism some patterns of my own struggles to humanize my environment. I trust that an ongoing dialogue with her will help me clarify my goals even further.

Dr. Mariam Mar'i, an educator from Acre, describes how, as a child, she became conscious of the people around her as mired in the passivity of waiting, the cult of waiting, the fear of breaking out of the spell. How many years had to pass by, how many humiliating incidents, how much refining of individual survival skills, how many changes in the world, before a new generation of Israeli-Palestinian leaders could emerge? When I listen to her I am reminded of the spiritual growth of my family and my people. I experience dialogue as the meeting of multidimensional human beings, and the most significant dimension is recurrent change and reevaluation.

Israel's history evolved in a direction that pushed the possibility of dialogue with Arabs to mere fantasy.

In 1967, the Six Day War triggered an occasion for "applied messianism." It came to a peak following the blow of the Yom Kippur War, when Israelis of all types felt a sore need for revision. Secular Zionism renewed itself through the protest wave that matured into the Democratic Movement for Change, while religious Zionists founded Gush Emunim ("the Block of the Faithful"):

> We have been commanded to inherit the land which God, may He be exalted, gave to our forefathers, Abraham, Isaac, and Jacob, and not to leave it in the hands of other nations nor [leave it] desolate. . . . Similarly . . . if our tribes wish to leave it and conquer for themselves the land of Shin'ar or Assyria or other places, they are not permitted [to do so]. . . . This is a positive commandment for poster-

ity, incumbent upon each one of us even during the period
of exile.

This is the reference often used by Gush Emunim: Nachman-
ides, a biblical commentator, scholar, and kabbalist, who resided
in Spain in the thirteenth century.

By insisting on the religious duty to settle in the parts of the
historic homeland contested by its present Arab inhabitants,
"the faithful" exercise the age-old art of creative interpretation
on several levels. First, from all biblical episodes they choose to
be inspired by the merciless conquest of Canaan by Joshua.
Second, from all rabbinical authorities they select as binding
legal tradition the one that sanctions active inheritance of the
land regardless of prevailing historical realities. And third, from
all the different trends within present-day Zionism, they claim
to be the legitimate heirs of the revered pioneers.

When we engage in dialogue it is not enough to state that we
disagree with such views. The peace movement can succeed only
if we learn to create innovative perspectives with our Palestinian
partners. If we come to the task of peacemaking with all the
richness of our tradition, we may be better equipped for inspiring solutions. For instance, the Peace Now movement was
started in Israel in 1978, following Egyptian President Sadat's
commendable breakthrough of the deadlock of enmity. It thrived
on the ensuing fears that the Likud government was imprisoned
in a mind-set that was going to kill the peace process. Ever since
then, the bulk of the Israeli peace movement has concentrated
its efforts along the same line — protest groups that cry out, on
the one hand, against abuse of human and civil rights, and on
the other hand point at the government's unwillingness to take
the necessary steps toward a political solution. Not enough
thought has been invested in drafting alternative modes of relating to Arabs based on our tradition. When I engage in dialogical
meetings with Palestinians, I try to break out of the depressing
Sisyphean mode of protest, toward a positive, optimistic activity
with its uplifting moments of pure hope. I believe that if we can
talk to each other, our leaders can also do it around the negotiating table.

The religious peace movement was established earlier than Peace Now, in 1975, as a protest against Gush Emunim's claim to monopoly over updated interpretation of national myths. Oz Ve'Shalom ("Strength and Peace," a comforting formula that the secular moderate liberals discovered only years later with their "Council for Security and Peace") borrowed a phrase from the daily liturgy for its name, and reminded the public that classic Judaism, as crystalized by the rabbis after the destruction of the second temple in 70 C.E., carefully sublimated ancient biblical war stories into irrelevance:

Abba Sikra, the leader of the Zealots of Jerusalem, was the nephew of Rabbi Yohanan son of Zakai. Rabbi Yohanan called for him in secrecy and demanded: "How long will you continue with your rebelliousness which perpetuates the Roman siege, and kill everyone with hunger?" Said the nephew: "What shall I do, if I say anything they will kill me." Said Rabbi Yohanan: "Give me an idea how I can get out of here, maybe I can save some." Said he: "Pretend you are ill, and everyone will come to see you, and put something that stinks near you, and they will say you died, and have only your loyal students carry you out to be buried." So he did. When they arrived at the city gates, the Jewish soldiers wanted to check him by spearing him and shaking him. The students begged: "Don't do this, lest they say you showed your Rabbi disrespect!" They opened the gate and let him out.

When he arrived at the Roman camp, he said to the commander Vespasian: "Hail the King!" Said Vespasian: "You deserve two deaths: one, for calling me king, which I am not, and the second, if I am king, why have you not come before to pay your respect?" Said Rabbi Yohanan: "You are king, because the mighty Jerusalem can only fall in the hands of a king, and I have not come before because the Zealots have not let me come."

Meanwhile, a messenger came and announced that the Caesar had died and the leaders of Rome had voted to nominate Vespasian as heir. Said Vespasian: "I have to leave this place and send someone else, but first ask for something and I will grant it." Said Rabbi Yohanan: "Give me the town of Yavne and its sages, and the dynasty of Rabbi Gamliel, and physicians to cure Rabbi Zadok." And so it was.

Years later, Rav Yosef, or maybe Rabbi Akiva, criticized him: "He should have asked him to spare Jerusalem." But Rabbi Yohanan thought that there was no chance such a wish could be granted, and that he would have missed the opportunity to save what little he could.

As this story shows, the destruction cannot be blamed solely on outside enemies like the Romans. When leaders—Jewish, Palestinian, the analogy works for both—mistakenly assess a historical circumstance as ripe for a messianic outburst, when they become falsely inspired by supposed prophetic zeal and ignore the necessary compromise that arouses out of our human condition, usually nothing but destruction can ensue.

I was attracted to Oz Ve'Shalom because I longed for an inspiring ideology that combines warm communality with a practical approach to the heterogenous population of the land—religious and secular, Ashkenazi and Sephardi, Jewish and Arab, Jewish, Muslim, and Christian. Years later I met Avner Amiel, an experienced community worker deeply committed to the promotion of democracy and peace in the Katamon neighborhood of Jerusalem, which is—like the development town of Yeruham where I chose to reside and to realize Zionism—predominantly populated by Jews from Islamic countries with strong traditional tendencies. "We must respect their tribal mentality," he said, "and present the message of peace and coexistence through the myths of sages like Rabbi Yohanan son of Zakai. Religious Jews understand the longing for a home of one's own, and that is what we have to stress; we should call upon their empathy for the plight of the stateless Palestinians, and at the same time reinforce their pride in their own communities and traditions."

It is my impression that Palestinians find it easier to dialogue with Jews who have adopted a Westernized, liberal version of Judaism, which is based on the reduction of Judaism to a religion only—that is, faith and practice of the individual, or even rituals of the voluntary congregation. Philosophies such as non-Zionist secular Judaism (Chomsky, Deutcher), secular Israeli liberalism (the Movement for Citizens' Rights, "Ratz"), anti-Zionist ultra-Orthodoxy (Neturei Karta), or even a modern Orthodox scholar like Professor Yesha' aia Leibovitz who preaches in favor of total separation of state and institutional religion as well as total denial of any substantive holiness of the land—all of these are understandably more accessible. But we must see the Jewish-Arab dialogue as the clash of conflicting national aspirations, a clash that really hurts. Mainstream Judaism has always revolved around the axis of a nation-state as the ultimate heavenly inspired kingdom on earth, in the land of Israel, which is a contested land. Dialogues with Palestinians have taught me not only to respect the proud nationalism of my people's enemies, but also brought home a sense of the fear and anger that Zionism arouses in them. This is what needs to be faced, and it hurts, but it is like growing pains.

Thus, in coexistence, events where the official terminology adopted by both sides is "the Israeli people and the Palestinian people," I always insist on speaking of the Jewish people, Zionism, and the state of Israel. I come to the dialogue with all the complexities of my heritage, and I mistrust all attempts to simplify that heritage by adjusting to the definitions of the other side (or some third party—namely, the American civic tradition) for the sake of establishing a false symmetry. Since dialogue often includes, among other aspects, a contest of wills, I should rather explore the dimension of respective, distinctive cultures than the more tedious and irritating ground of who-has-suffered-more ("Can horror stories of 1948 or 1989 ever beat the Holocaust?"), or who-came-first ("How old is the Palestinian entity anyway?"). After all, it is no coincidence that the Israeli declaration of independence defines the right of the Jews to have a state of their own on the basis of the distinctive culture they created on the land, beginning with the Bible.

A creative dialogue, then, based on respect for national Judaism, is my aim, and perhaps religious Zionism is where it can grow beyond its present condition.

Nothing illustrates the need to outgrow our present limitations through consciousness raising better than an insight into the word "shalom" itself. In Hebrew (as well as in Arabic), "peace" connotes wholesomeness, perfection, which is why it is one of God's names. By contrast, the human condition has been understood as partial and imperfect, and therefore "peace" has evolved as a double-standard concept—a sublime, idealized abstraction, and a pragmatic political agenda.

Some texts reveal what kind of "peace" Jews thought they could realistically expect if they were both worthy and lucky:

> When you come near a city to make war against it, then you should call out to it in peace. And if it answers you in peace and opens the gates for you, then all the people found in it will be tributaries to you and will serve you. But if it does not make peace with you and wages war against you, then you will besiege it. And when the Lord your God delivers it into your hand, you shall smite every male with the edge of the sword. But the women and the children and the cattle and all that will be in the city and all the spoil you will take as booty, and you shall enjoy the spoil of your enemies which the Lord your God has given you. [Deut. 20:10–14]

Thus, in an adversarial, cruel world, the only way to secure the welfare and prosperity of a community is to convert foreign elements that interfere with homogeneity, or eliminate them, or suppress them into obedient submissiveness.

Utopia therefore can only be pictured as one big fortified castle:

> I rejoiced when they told me, let us go to the house of the Lord. Our feet were standing in your gates, Jerusalem. Jerusalem, which is built as a city where all associate together, where the tribes of the Lord go up, as a testimony for Israel, to give thanks unto the name of the Lord. For there were placed chairs for judgment, chairs for the dynasty of David. Pray for the peace of Jerusalem, may those who love you enjoy tranquility. May there be peace within your walls, tranquility in your palaces. For the sake of my brothers and friends let me speak, peace be within

you. For the sake of the house of the Lord our God, I will ask for your good. [Ps. 122]

In addition, many Jewish holidays (Passover, Purim, Hanukah, and even the modern Independence Day) record the historical experience of an oppressed people — that deliverance and salvation could be achieved only through victory and defeat of the enemy:

And the opposite happened, that the Jews had power over those who hate them. [Est. 9:1]

I can explain what gave rise to such mistrust of the other nations, but we must not remain bound by an ethic that defines security and pluralism as mutually exclusive. Dialogue between people of different nationalities is the tool to advance coexistence of equals.

Even the uplifting visions of the prophets about universal peace are insufficient for our purpose, because they are tainted by the same conceptual limitations — the end of wars shall come only when all nations unanimously accept the spiritual supremacy of God's message, as carried in the world by the people of Israel:

And it shall come to pass in the end of days, that the mountain of the Lord's house shall be firmly established on the top of the mountains . . . and unto it shall flow all the nations. And many people shall go and say: "Come and let us go up to the mountain of the Lord, to the house of the God of Jacob, that He may teach us His ways, and we may walk in His paths, for out of Zion shall go forth the Law and the word of God out of Jerusalem." And he will judge among the nations . . . and they shall beat their swords into plough-shares and their spears into pruning-knives, nation shall not lift up sword against nation and they shall not learn any more war. [Is. 2:2–4]

A popular Israeli song uses a familiar phrase from the liturgy:

He who makes peace in His heights will make peace for
us and for all of [the people of] Israel, and say Amen.

This is a prayer for a "separate peace" for the Jews only, and
the work of peacemaking is left to the omnipotent God, for the
kind of messianic peace that will transform the earth into a
reflection of heaven is certainly beyond our ken, here and now.
When belligerent right-wing Jews declare that all Jews want
peace, this is what they mean; even Rabbi Meir Kahane offered
a literally correct reading of some texts. But with the ancient,
well-perfected art of rabbinical creative interpretation, we can
and should expand shalom, toward faith in a dialogue that is
based on accepting and respecting the different reality of others
without demanding that they clone us first.

Dialogue provides both partners with an opportunity to
search their own traditions candidly and to develop a self-image
based on tolerance, without rejecting the different parts of their
heritage. I know that some Muslims may have a hard time promoting this effort now, because of the current surge of antidialogical fundamentalism.

I am excited by the potential contained in the biblical concept
of covenant, which in Hebrew is always "cut," as reflected also
in the accompanying ritual of circumcision, the setting aside or
cutting of animals, or the establishment of an actual border (e.g.,
Gen. 31:44–53). The purpose of the covenant, especially when
it is literally "cut between" unequal partners, is to establish
mutual respect of boundaries and sovereignty as a prerequisite
to mutual trust, cooperation, peace, and even love. With this in
mind, we can draw from the Torah the idea that sharing the
land to resolve a serious conflict is sometimes more important
than taking possession of the God-promised inheritance:

And there arose a strife between the shepherds of Abram's
cattle and the shepherds of Lot's cattle. . . . And Abram
said to Lot: "Let there be no strife between you and me
and between my shepherds and yours, for we are close
relatives. Is not the whole land before you? Please separate
from me, if you go left I will go to the right, and if you go

to the right, I will go to the left." . . . And they separated
from each other. [Gen. 13:7–11]

Only recently have Zionists, such as myself, religious or not,
come to accept the two-state solution as part of our peace plan.
This has evolved through dialogues with Palestinians who have
likewise come a long way to arrive at the same conclusion. The
peace movement developed as an inner Jewish dialogue, as a
dispute among ourselves about values and responsibility to the
future of the Jewish people. As late as a decade ago, many Jews
who worked with Arabs as political equals were excluded from
the Zionist consensus—the Communist Party, mavericks like Uri
Avneri, the legacy of Brit Shalom from the 1930s with its vision
of a binational state. Most of us remained engulfed in our own
drama and mythmaking, and saw the Arabs as an abstraction,
neither particularly hated nor really perceived as three-dimen-
sional human beings that comprise over one-sixth of the population inside the Green Line alone. We relegated them to a
stereotyped role in our own national drama—the enemy, the
obstacle to our secure independence. We in the women's movement have learned that when the ruling gender abstracts other
humans into a mere secondary role in the protagonists' drama—
the sex object, the mother, the untainted virgin—what ensues is
discrimination and confinement in the best of cases and downright abuse in the worst of them. The same can be said about
the mistreatment of Arabs by most Zionists—we have not fully
seen them. Now we do, and this calls for dialogue.

In many instances, the weaker parties in society engage in
dialogues with their allies or their opponents, only because they
have nothing to lose, no power to concede, no violent or adversarial strategies to unlearn. I think that this is why there are so
many more women, Jewish and Palestinian, who are involved in
dialogue now; we are as yet politically weaker than our men and
therefore better disposed for alternative political activities at a
time when government fails to move history onward. But women
are not more dialogical in their nature than are men—the real
task is to humanize politics, to work toward empowerment but
at the same time to ensure that empowerment does not entail
a stiffening of the dialogical disposition.

In summary, here are two examples of creative bridges between ancient religious wisdom and new realities in the land we must share with another people.

My desert hometown Yeruham has only two Arab families — a Bedouin who served in the Israeli army and married a woman from Gaza, and a doctor from Galilee who works in our health clinic; his wife is a nursery school teacher. Thirty-three Bedouin families live in tents on the hills nearby, grazing sheep and paying lawyers to fight off the government's claim to ownership of their lands. When they are harassed by the Green Patrol (a special police force set up to control open spaces) they come to me for help — to argue with the authorities, call the lawyers, alarm the press. Once I worked hard to bail out five young men who had been unjustly arrested. When it was all over, my ten-year-old foster daughter asked: "Is this the meaning of the daily prayer — 'Blessed be thou, our God, king of the universe, who releases prisoners'?"

Most Jews have no doubt uttered this ancient prayer in conjunction with their own deliverance from unjust imprisonment at the hand of anti-Semites, but this little girl, exposed to ratification of injustice of the Israeli system, felt equally connected to her religious education and was thus moved toward an original reinterpretation of the text.

I have recently experienced a similar expansion of my heritage when I prepared for a joint lecture tour through North America, sponsored by the New Israel Fund, with Dr. Mariam Mar'i. As I was grasping for a term that could best summarize why I feel so close to this woman, across the obvious differences between us, someone volunteered: "Here you are, two Halutzot [pioneer women]." Quite so. In the Bible, the "pioneers" were brave soldiers who led the battle of conquest (Num. 32:17–32). In modern times, "pioneers" were brave Jews who realized Zionist goals ahead of the hesitant people, came to the land of Israel, settled in remote outposts, and toiled the barren soil. As an educator and activist I attempt to break new ground along the front of social justice: I have spent years trying to preach this kind of lifework as the most pressing "pioneering" challenge of this generation. And this is exactly what Mariam, an Israeli Palestinian, does on her side. Perhaps this is the ultimate meaning of dialogue—to reach out to Mariam and learn how to lead our communities toward the pioneer work of joint building of the land.

REFERENCES FOR FURTHER READING

Fred David Levine, *Territory or Peace? Religious Zionism in Conflict.* Institute on American Jewish-Israeli Relations, the American Jewish Committee, New York, 1986. A short, well documented summary, with bibliography.

Oz Ve'Shalom—Netivot Shalom, English-language publications by the Jewish religious peace movement, *Religious Zionism: Challenges and Choices. Jerusalem, 1984.*

———, *Violence and the Value of Life in Jewish Tradition.* Jerusalem, 1984.

———, *Torah Against Terror.* Jerusalem, 1984.

4

The Basic Principles of Dialogue in the Israeli-Palestine Conflict: Respect, Honesty, Sincerity, Humility

NAIM STIFAN ATEEK

Dialogue is a challenging encounter with a purpose. It cannot be an end itself, nor should it be cyclical. At its best, dialogue is linear, constantly moving, though at times in a zigzagging fashion, but definitely moving toward an objective. Dialogue could be terminated along the way, and it could start again. It could lead its participants back to square one. But true dialogue is hopeful and draws interlocutors closer together.

In the Middle East, although there have been certain forms of dialogue and some limited progress has been made, tangible consequences of achieving peace are still not clearly in sight. The progress that has been made thus far has dealt with peripheral issues, leaving the core of the conflict untouched.

As I write this article, I should like to make two observations. On the one hand, we are living in the last decade of the twentieth century. The Israel-Palestine conflict has been ideologically with us throughout this century. The second half of this century witnessed the tragedy of Palestine and the uprooting of the

Palestinians, while the first half witnessed the tragedy of the Holocaust and the annihilation of one-third of the Jewish people. Consequently, many Jews immigrated to Palestine. The aspirations of the two peoples and their definitions of what constituted a life of freedom, security, and peace conflicted. The view of one side was based most often on the denial and negation of the other. Dialogue between the two was either nonexistent or frustrated when attempted. Today, these two peoples continue to be interlocked with strife and are still very much apart.

On the other hand, one observes a movement toward conflict resolution in the world. There is a growing feeling that the changes on the world scene and the new leadership of the superpowers provide real opportunities to find solutions to some of the more intractable international problems. We have seen rapprochement between Iran and Iraq, the South Africans and SWAPO in Namibia. Furthermore, the Soviets are pulling out of Afghanistan, radical change is sweeping through Eastern Europe, and Nelson Mandela is now free. These are encouraging signs.

The *intifada* has awakened people throughout the world to the desperate plight of the Palestinians, so there is a ray of hope that the Israel-Palestine conflict, which has seen many bad days of spiraling violence, may be on the verge of being redirected into a path that will lead to peace. I am writing this article to emphasize the basic principles that should undergird any dialogue between Palestinians and Israeli Jews. It is important to point to certain dangers, so that they can be avoided and to emphasize the genuine possibility of the achievement of peace in our region.

The Israel-Palestine conflict was political in its initial phases. Originally, this conflict resulted from the claims of two peoples for exclusive right to the same land. Each side presented convincing arguments to support its position, each side claiming historical rights and roots. Since then, religious elements have come to play an important role. Today, the religious and political aspects of this struggle are inseparable for some. Western Christian fundamentalists, Jewish fundamentalists, and some Western liberals have used religious arguments to buttress Jewish claims to the land, thus hoping that Palestinians would simply accept this as a divine verdict and supinely relinquish their claim.

One would hope that when the two parties come together for negotiations and dialogue, it would be possible to separate the political nature of the conflict from the religious, which has increasingly become emotionally explosive. Some religious groups will certainly do their utmost to interject their beliefs into the process. The hope, however, is that the political aspect of the conflict will be treated as its core and that negotiators will not succumb to the pressure of religious zealots.

I was encouraged as the struggle between Egypt and Israel over Taba unfolded. Taba is a small strip of land that Israel retained when it returned the Sinai to Egypt as stipulated by the Camp David accords. Egypt claimed that Taba should also be returned to it. After much haggling, the case was turned over for arbitration to the International Court of Justice (The Hague), which appointed a committee of judges to decide the case. A few years later, the judges ruled that Taba should be returned to Egypt. Even though the Israeli government was not pleased with the ruling, it complied.

During the Taba case, one would hear arguments in favor of Israel's claim that were quite emotionally provocative. People would say, "Look at how large Egypt is in comparison to Israel!" Or they would say, "Look at how much territory Israel gave back to Egypt when it returned Sinai. How can Egypt still insist on a one mile stretch of territory?" Obviously, the judges did not consider such trite arguments. They based their decisions on the legal rights of the claimants.

This is very heartening. The problem, obviously, is that Taba is far away and does not constitute, for any Jew, an integral part of Eretz Yisrael. One of the most delicate things that must be done, therefore, if dialogue is to succeed, is to untangle religious elements from the political ones. That is why, I believe, that Israel, after receiving international legitimacy from the U.N. in 1948, has refused to allow the U.N. to resolve the conflict. To go back to the U.N. would effectively mean that Israel would have to submit itself to international law, which judges on the basis of legal right and wrong.

Admittedly, the political and religious factors have become today so intertwined that some would say that to separate them is to deny Israel one of its strongest arguments and give the advantage to the Palestinians. It seems, therefore, only wishful thinking on the part of some Palestinians to separate religion from politics. I am sure that there will be those in the Jewish community who will claim that there are certain religious imperatives that outweigh all others. It can, therefore, be argued that God is the principal obstacle to peace — God as perceived by these religious people. God is being invoked to substantiate the claim of one side over the other in such a way that peace cannot come about. Clearly, although the conflict was originally wholly political, it soon ceased to be so. It is my own view that the religious element is the most volatile aspect of the conflict and could prove to be the greatest obstacle to peace in the region.

Dialogue is a Western phenomenon, a Western concept, and it has become an accepted way for individuals, peoples, and nations to resolve conflicts. Although it is very important, it is interesting to examine how people have always lived together in the Middle East. Western-style dialogue is not unknown, but conflict resolution is a highly developed art that is practiced regularly.

Throughout history, a wide variety of peoples, nations, and communities have mingled in the Middle East. Since the seventh century C.E., Palestine has been the land where three religious communities — Jews, Christians, and Muslims — have lived side by side. In some places, they lived in separate sections of towns, but these were not ghettos imposed by some hostile authority. In fact, they were seen as healthy phenomena where one could live with one's coreligionists. There was always a great deal of social mixing, but social relationships never included intermarriage. Marriage was sacrosanct and was possible only within one's own community. Mixed marriages between persons belonging to different religions were looked down upon and most often the life of the offenders was threatened. When feuds erupted between the religious communities, due to economic, political, or religious tension, the leaders of the communities would come together quickly to settle the conflict according to

Middle Eastern customs and traditions. These customs still function in many places in the Middle East. Friendships, however, were always formed across religious boundaries.

People lived together with a good deal of respect and tolerance. They avoided religious discussions as much as possible, though religious questions were raised and answered among friends. It was felt that the best insurance for maintaining friendship and peace was achieved by a clear avoidance of religious issues. There were times, however, when religious fanatics from one or other of the communities would ignite the flames of religious intolerance and bigotry. Or when a nonreligious strife was given a religious connotation, it thus became immediately inflammable. Such strife almost invariably brought the greatest hardship on the minority community or communities. The prominent men of the community were always quick to deal with such matters. They had to remain constantly alert to prevent the recurrence of such communal strife. All in all, it might be said that the three religious communities coexisted with relatively few problems and a good measure of relative harmony.

One cannot use the word *dialogue* to describe the relationship that existed between the different religious communities throughout many periods of our Middle East history. Dialogue is a modern phenomenon, and a mainly Western concept. In the Middle East people learned to live together. The concrete practicalities of daily life obliged constant relationships with each other. Life together was a practical, key concept for the religious communities. Life was lived fully within certain known and accepted limits and boundaries. Those who stepped beyond those boundaries hurt themselves and most often contributed to the hurt of others.

Today as we confront the Middle East conflict, its apparent complexity has erased the simplicity of life that long existed and the time-honored ways of dealing with communal strife. Outsiders press us to engage in Western-style dialogue as a means for achieving a solution. Dialogue, as someone suggested, is:

> A sustained conversation between parties who are not saying the same thing and who recognize and respect the differences, the contradictions, and the mutual exclusions

between their various ways of thinking. The object of this dialogue is understanding and appreciation, leading to further reflection upon the implication for one's own position of the convictions ... appreciation must precede reconciliation of ideas.[1]

This is a good definition of what dialogue should be. Although it is not a part of our tradition, Palestinians can, I believe, engage in it creatively. It is important, however, to watch out so that dialogue will not deteriorate into an artificial and academic activity between two estranged groups.

For us in the Middle East, the only real and viable dialogue is that which goes beyond formal meetings into the real-life relationships of people together. Living together as neighbors, day by day, is the key to a future of peace for our people—a future where enmities gradually diminish and friendships steadily grow. Such a future demands new realism on the part of Palestinians and Israelis. It also demands a new basis that can govern both the process of dialogue as well as the daily life of people of community.

Before dialogue is possible, both sides—Palestinians and Israeli Jews—must become more realistic. In retrospect, it is clear that, in the past, both have misunderstood and underestimated each other. Palestinians underestimated the power and organization of world Jewry, and the determination of the Zionist Jews to take and inhabit Palestine, or part of it. Palestinians have also not realized the formidable role the Holocaust played in making the Zionist dream a reality. Jews have underestimated the will of Palestinians to achieve their right of self-determination and nationhood, and to move decisively in that direction in a relatively short period of time.

More and more, one notices that this lack of realism is fading away. Although both sides still cling to fantastic dreams, the atmosphere created by this growing realism is conducive to peace. One can almost feel the birth pangs of an authentic dialogue: it is about to be born. Any residual elements of fantasy must be dissipated. Dialogue can be hampered when leading Israelis and Palestinians continue to advocate a "Greater Israel" or a "Greater Palestine."[2] Fantasies will continue to flourish in the mind of fanatics and extremists of both sides. They will create havoc because they refuse to bow to the facts. They will remain hostage to their own fantasies. Denial of reality is the mortal enemy of dialogue. As we appeal for the end of fantasy and approach the birth of dialogue, we need to call attention to certain dangers that need to be avoided.

Dialogue should not be used as camouflage. This is a real danger in the Middle East. Dialogue in this way becomes opportunity to silence the people who originally demanded it. It is a way of pretending to deal with the issues at hand while not actually discussing them. Dialogue, in other words, should never be allowed to become an end in itself. It should not be used by one party to buy time. Camouflage can be used to call into question the other party's intention so as to frustrate the dialogue process and blame it on the other. Such underlying deceptions will eventually become apparent, but it is important to point them out from the outset.

Dialogue should not be used as a way of escaping the real issues of the conflict. There is an important difference between using dialogue as an escape and using it as camouflage. The latter carries with it an element of deception. The former implies a willful avoidance of the central issues by wasting time on the periphery.

Dialogue should not be used for propaganda. It is easy for dialogue to be hijacked by one side and used for propaganda purposes. Any party behaving in such a way is clearly not sincere, and endangers the peace process. By refraining from propagandizing, the participants give the dialogue a chance to move forward.

Furthermore, dialogue should not be used to keep minorities—ethnic, religious, or otherwise—in check. It is very sinister and devious when the stronger party uses dialogue to find out the thoughts and feelings of weaker groups in order to exploit and control them. As I shall discuss later, openness is an important ingredient to true dialogue, but this openness should not be used against anyone. Interlocutors should not be punished for their candor.

Dialogue should not, under the banner of "democracy," be

used as a tool for repression. It is part of the contradiction in the present conflict that one of the parties of dialogue can claim to be democratic and yet not respond to the conflict democratically. The existence of democracy within a state is not a guarantee that a conflict will be solved on democratic grounds. A state can pride itself on its democratic nature, while in practice continue to oppress and control people against their will. Democracy becomes a comfortable self-deceptive banner rather than a means of facing and solving issues of injustice. To allow people to cry for justice and freedom, and not to respond to their cry, is perhaps nearly as repressive as denying them the right to speak, and certainly creates special forms of pain.

Dialogue should not be entered into with the dominator/dominated mentality, which assumes that the stronger side will behave as it is accustomed to behaving and impose constraints on the dialogue. No positive results can be achieved if the dominant party is imposing its prior conditions, which undercut the full rights of the dominated. In the Israel-Palestine conflict, the dialogue will not be genuine if the Palestinians are denied the right to choose their own representatives. To be forced to accept the terms of the stronger party ensures end results that only the stronger party can accept, thus making a sham of the basic presuppositions of free dialogue. The only precondition to genuine dialogue is the acceptance of the full humanity of the other. No dialogue is possible when one's right to existence as a free human being is denied.

Because pressure is mounting on both the state of Israel and the Palestinians to meet, it is important to identify certain principles, which, if applied, would further the movement of authentic dialogues and bring about a greater measure of justice and peace in the Middle East. I should like to introduce these principles by two personal experiences.

In 1984 I was invited to attend the International Council of Christians and Jews (ICCJ) in Holland. In a small discussion group, I suggested that one way out of the political impasse was to have Palestinian Christians and Jews face each other with mutual confessions of wrongs committed by one against the other. I specifically asked the secretary of the group to relate my suggestion to the plenary.

When the secretary neglected to do that, I insistently stood up and supplemented his report. I noted that after World War II, a number of Christian churches and groups in the West issued statements confessing their guilt and negligence for not having acted decisively enough to prevent the Holocaust. These groups sought to move forward in solidarity with the Jews. I also observed that these statements greatly improved the relationship between many Christians and Jews and helped to open lines of communication between them. Since we were meeting as religious people and not as politicians, I went on to say, it would be appropriate for us to look each other in the eye and confess our guilt against one another. This would be a good exercise that might catch on and ultimately reach the leadership of both the Israelis and the Palestinians.

After I spoke in the plenary, it was as though a bomb had exploded in the hall. Men and women, mostly from the Jewish participants, stood up to attack me. Some tried to discredit me. One woman angrily and emotionally explained that there is no confession in Judaism. She added that the Jews had done nothing wrong to the Palestinians, and thus there could be no confession.

I have often reflected on that difficult experience. It is essential, I believe, that people in conflict admit their own history even when it is painful. When conflicts are prolonged and enmities deepen, it is not possible for one party to claim absolute right. That is why the essential elements of dialogue have to do with mutual acceptance, the willingness of both sides to listen to each other, and above all the moral courage of both sides to confess to "the other" the wrongs done to the other. This experience reflects the depths of self-justification and the resistance most people have to positive confrontations, which are key elements to conflict resolution. I still believe that such a litany of confession could serve as the basis for an Israeli-Palestinian dialogue.[3]

The other experience happened in 1980 in Haifa when the Interfaith Association, then called the Interfaith Committee in Israel, tried to organize interfaith activities in Haifa and the vicinity. For a number of years, such activity was taking place in Jerusalem, and the committee wanted to extend it to other parts of the country. Three persons were asked to speak at this inaugural meeting: a Jewish professor from the Hebrew University in Jerusalem who was the chairman of the Interfaith Committee, a Muslim qadi of Acre, and myself. At this meeting, I described four basic ingredients or principles for interfaith dialogue. I believe that these principles are relevant not only to interfaith dialogue, but to any dialogue, including that between Israelis and Palestinians when they meet for the resolution of the conflict. These four are as follows:

1. *Respect.* Respect is the first important ingredient for successful dialogue. It has two dimensions. Participants must be mature, knowledgeable, having self-respect and integrity. Weak individuals who lack self-respect are obstacles to healthy dialogue. Participants must also respect the integrity of the other party. This implies obedience to the Golden Rule, "In everything, do to others what you would have them do to you" (Matt. 7:12). The same principle was enunciated by Rabbi Hillel: "what is hateful to you, do not to your companion."[4] Respect keeps the other party's interest in mind. It should lead to mutual respect. And mutual respect should lead to mutual acceptance of the personhood of the other. Respect and acceptance do not rule out one party's challenging the other, but respect should lead each party to change its attitude toward the other. Respect makes it possible for each party to understand and speak to the other party's deepest needs.

In the final analysis, justice itself is an act of respect for God the Creator and for our fellow human beings. To resist injustice becomes, therefore, an obligation that each person in dialogue must accept. It is a way of valuing human beings.[5]

2. *Fairness, Honesty, and Fidelity to Truth.* Another basic ingredient to successful dialogue is fidelity to truth. In the Middle East, deception and denial of truth have carried the day. Some have believed that the only way to survive is to hide the truth and protect duplicity. Fidelity to truth is often seen as a luxury that many national leaders cannot afford.

In the Israel-Palestine conflict, it is important to emphasize the need for Israelis and Palestinians to confront each other with truth. To tell the truth requires openness, and openness allows them to speak frankly, yet sensitively.

To speak truthfully will also help dispel the fear and distrust that so blind the two communities. The Israelis have deep fears that come from long centuries of history. These have been compounded with new fears, which have been intensified since the beginning of the conflict with clichés like "the Arabs want only to push the Jews into the sea."[6]

The Palestinians have their own fears also. Their national aspirations have been denied by Israel.[7] Israel continues to confiscate their land and threaten their identity. This has not created a climate of trust. On the contrary, it has enhanced distrust and deepened fears. A commitment to truth is absolutely necessary in order to allay the fears and to create an atmosphere conducive to dialogue.

Fidelity to truth also involves addressing the core issues without wasting unnecessary time on the periphery, and with a minimum of wrangling on questions of format, structure, and shape. In the Israel-Palestine conflict, both sides have emphasized the need for peace, but each approached it from a different angle. Jews seek peace with security. The Palestinians have long sought peace with justice. Fairness implies a commitment to the demands of security and justice for both peoples. In other words, there must be peace that is just for the Palestinians and secure for the Israelis. There should be a peace that lessens the fear and augments the trust.

Another aspect of honesty is a correct assessment of the past. Honesty neither shrinks from nor becomes obsessed with the past. It assesses and evaluates, learns and moves ahead. Honesty does not use past injustices to shackle either interlocutor nor does it exploit the past in order to impose unnecessary demands on the other.

One feels that some Jews have exploited the Holocaust to prolong and deepen the guilt of others and to avoid honest criticism of the state of Israel. Honesty shuns such endeavors. It recognizes that humans are capable of evil, and it does not justify injustice with further injustice.

3. *Sincerity.* Dialogue should not degenerate into mere intellectual activity. It should be a serious activity that involves the

whole person. That is why I began this article by saying that dialogue at its best must not move in circles, nor should it cherish vacuum in order to consume time. It is sincere in its commitment to reach its objectives as fast and as effectively as it can without undue delay. Sincerity in dialogue means that interlocutors move as quickly as possible because they realize that the level of suffering among the common folk, who usually bear the brunt of a conflict, is reduced when a conflict is quickly resolved. At the same time, sincerity means a commitment to details so that no corners of injustice are cut short and no issues relating to the conflict are left unclarified. Everything is done in order to prevent the germination of any new seeds of enmity between the parties.

Above all, sincerity, like honesty, implies the integrity to take the needs of the other into account and find adequate answers for them. It does not imply stubbornness and inflexibility, but the willingness to see and empathize with the legitimate needs of the other and do whatever one can to address them. In the Israel-Palestine conflict, as in other places of conflict, sincerity is very crucial. The relationships between Palestinians and Jews have been marred so often as a result of insincerity. Both honesty and sincerity are sure ingredients for restoring confidence and trust between the two parties.

4. *Humility.* Humility is one of the most essential ingredients in dialogue and negotiations and genuine dialogue cannot exist without it. The failure of dialogue is often the result of arrogance. One cannot sit around the table of dialogue with the attitude that the other side is completely wrong and one's own side is totally right. That kind of arrogance has no place where genuine dialogue is pursued and where people are working toward reaching a peaceful settlement between enemies. Humility insures that interlocutors approach each other with openness to the different possibilities that will present themselves along the way.

Moreover, one cannot approach dialogue with the feeling of superiority over the other, a sense of higher morality, or even the feeling of self-sufficiency. The key to a permanent peace in Israel-Palestine does not lie in the total separation of the two peoples in conflict, but in their ultimate interrelatedness to each other and their interdependence. Humility insures such a change in attitude. People would no longer see each other as conqueror/conquered, oppressor/oppressed, victimizer/victimized, but as human beings who have both suffered in the period of conflict. Their new interdependence puts them on a new road that will lead them to undo the harm that has been done and to create the necessary institutions for the reconciliation and healing of people.

Having said that, it does not mean that the difference between victim and victimizer is blurred or should quickly be abolished. One should not deny or gloss over the responsibility of the oppressor to the oppressed. Nor is it right to pretend that differences do not matter. They do and it should be clear where the responsibilities lie. Things should be rightly named and correctly labeled. But neither does it mean that when a settlement is reached and peace is achieved, the victim should forever hold the victimizer as a hostage. People should learn from the painful past, but also go beyond it so that life with all its positive possibilities will remain open for all involved.

The above four ingredients are essential if dialogue is to succeed. To these I would like to add two further ingredients from Paulo Freire, the author of *The Pedagogy of the Oppressed*.[8]

1. Dialogue requires a profound love for the world and for people. Love is the foundation of dialogue and it cannot exist if the relationship is that of domination:

> Domination reveals the pathology of love: sadism in the dominator and masochism in the dominated. Because love is an act of courage, not of fear, love is commitment to other men. No matter where the oppressed are found, the act of love is commitment to their cause—the cause of liberation. And this commitment, because it is loving, is dialogical. As an act of bravery, love cannot be sentimental; as an act of freedom, it must not serve as a pretext for manipulation. It must generate other acts of freedom; otherwise, it is not love. Only by abolishing the situation of oppression is it possible to restore the love which that situation made impossible. If I do not love the world—if I

do not love life—if I do not love men—I cannot enter into dialogue.[9]

2. Faith in human beings is the other requirement for dialogue, according to Freire:

Faith in man is an "a priori" requirement for dialogue; the "dialogical man" believes in other men even before he meets them face to face. His faith, however, is not naive. The "dialogical man" is critical and knows that although it is within the power of men to create and transform, in a concrete situation of alienation men may be impaired in the use of that power. Far from destroying his faith in man, however, this possibility strikes him as a challenge to which he must respond. He is convinced that the power to create and transform, even when thwarted in concrete situations, tends to be reborn. And that rebirth can occur—not gratuitously, but in and through the struggle for liberation. ... Without this faith in man, dialogue is a farce which inevitably degenerates into paternalistic manipulation.[10]

As we hope that the last decade of the twentieth century will be crowned by the true prospects of peace in Israel-Palestine, I hope that the above principles and ingredients of peace will be accepted as essential components for the dialogical relationship that will develop between Israelis and Palestinians. A peace process based on such a foundation will, undoubtedly, insure the desired results of justice, peace, and security for all the people of our area.

NOTES

1. John V. Taylor, "The Theological Basis of Interfaith Dialogue," in *Mission Trends No. 5*, Gerald H. Anderson and Thomas F. Stransky, eds. (New York: Paulist Press, 1981), p. 94.

2. In a documentary shown recently on Israeli television, a leading peace advocate in Jerusalem told of being asked how big a state of Israel he wanted and he answered, "Oh, I want a very big state—I want a state that stretches from Paris to Tokyo." The questioner then said,

"But, that is impossible!" The speaker then replied, "Ah yes, you are quite right—so it is. So let us now discuss what is possible."

3. During the First World War, Turks massacred Armenians. Armenian estimates are that 50 percent of their people were killed in cold blood. So far the Turks have not yet admitted that these tragic events took place. This failure to admit even the fact of this historical reality is understandably very painful for Armenians. What hope for meaningful dialogue would there be between white Americans and Native Americans if the white participants insisted on denying that the "Indians" were never massacred in the eighteenth and nineteenth centuries and that "Wounded Knee" never took place? Or what if the Germans categorically denied that the Holocaust ever took place and that all talk about it was evidence of Jewish hatred for Germans? Such a denial would also be unspeakably painful for the Jewish people. Although not of the same intensity, this is the same kind of pain that the Palestinians have endured for more than forty years.

4. B. T. Shab. 31a.

5. John Shea, *Stories of God* (Chicago: Thomas More Press, 1978), p. 114.

6. Some demagogues in the Arab camp talked that way in the heat of the prelude to the war of 1967. Such language is not used today. To think and act today on the basis of language spoken in passion twenty-three years ago (and since rejected) is irresponsible.

7. The U.N. vote that legitimized that state of Israel in 1948 also called for a Palestinian state.

8. Paulo Freire, *Pedagogy of the Oppressed* (New York: Continuum, 1970).

9. Ibid., p. 78.

10. Ibid., p. 79.

SECTION 3

TESTIMONIES OF LAWYERS

In Felicia Langer's small law office in Jerusalem—before she closed the office so as to sit down and write her memoirs—hang three pictures of young, smiling, dark-haired Palestinian girls. All three are named Felicia. At birth their parents had named them thus, so that they would daily remember Felicia Langer's difficult struggle for them in the Israeli courts. The three young Felicias now write regularly to Felicia Langer, telling her about their lives. We suspect that these three smiling Felicias are probably the only Palestinian girls in the world today named after a live Jewish woman.

Ziad Abu Zayad's law office in East Jerusalem is also the editorial and publishing office of *Gesher*, the only Palestinian newspaper that appears in Hebrew. Ziad Abu Zayad is the editor and publisher of this biweekly, which attempts to bring to the Jewish Israeli public, in their language, the Palestinian response to major developments in the Middle East. He subsidizes the newspaper from his lectures to Israelis in Hebrew on the need for Israelis to accept the legitimate rights of the Palestinian nation.

Clearly both these lawyers are exceptional. Their striving for justice and their quest for dialogue are very rare in a profession whose members supposedly should be sensitive to justice and to the abuse of civil and human rights. According to an ancient Jewish legend, the world is daily saved from destruction by the existence of thirty-six hidden *Zadikim*, righteous men who pursue justice. From what we know about the response of Israeli lawyers to blatant acts of injustice against Palestinians in Israel and in the occupied territories, we fear that among the many thousands of Jewish lawyers practicing in Israel today it would be extremely difficult to find thirty-six men and women who are struggling for justice because they care, not because they have an ax to grind.

Felicia Langer and Ziad Abu Zayad care. They express their striving for justice in their essays. For years they have worked within the military law system prevailing in the occupied territories, trying to uphold a semblance of justice. Most frequently they failed. They know that their struggle is Sisyphean, yet they continue. In order to show how frustrating such a struggle can be, we asked Felicia Langer to briefly relate one of the more difficult recent cases with which she dealt. She included the story of Al-Mator's brutal and unexplained death. We feel that it is a story in which the Israel Supreme Court wrongly supported an oppressive system that clearly abused justice. This story reveals the legal obstacles daily confronting the few lawyers who care and who authentically struggle for basic human rights in Israel.

Yet the following essays are not works of legal experts. They are primarily personal testimonies of two persons who wish to promote dialogue and justice in this troubled area of the world. The fact that they are lawyers only helps to sharpen their perspective in addressing some of the basic difficulties that such dialogue faces. Perhaps it also leads to some blind spots. But these blind spots are transcended by the authentic quest for dialogue, by the personal approach to members of the other nation, by the wish to find a just solution to our difficult situation.

5

The Pursuit of Justice and Dialogue: Israeli Persecution of Palestinians

FELICIA LANGER

I do not want to begin this article with a description of the trampling upon the human rights of Palestinians by the Israeli establishment, including the ministers of the Israeli Labor Party, which announces that as a socialist party it firmly believes in human rights. Nor do I want to begin with the unheralded and much too often unheard of terrible suffering of Palestinians under Israeli military rule. I have documented numerous examples of this uncalled for suffering in my books, the most recent of them is *An Age of Stone*.[1] Nor do I want to begin my writing with a description of my long years of difficult work for Palestinian human rights in the Israeli courts since 1967, years when I was ignored and often hated by most of my compatriots in Israel, because I spoke out against oppression of the Palestinian people and against the travesty of justice when dealing with Palestinians. I fear that starting in any one of these ways could be interpreted as antidialogical. So I want to start from something simple, seemingly neutral, something that does not reflect much of the bitterness, the frustration, and the sadness that I daily feel. Yes, let me start with the pursuit of justice.

I am a lawyer. For me being a lawyer is a calling, a vocation, a way of life; it is an aspiration to use my knowledge of the law to help ensure that more than a semblance of justice will prevail. (It sounds so simple that I blush at having to write these sentences.) I refuse to admire the cult of success that often prevails in this profession and which is often based on empty eloquence and callous cleverness. Maybe this attitude has helped me to succeed at times in my struggles—not financially, of course. This attitude has also led me to believe in dialogue and to work for it.

I should stress that my belief in dialogue emerged as a result of my activities in defense of human rights. After the 1967 war, when Israel began to rule hundreds of thousands of Palestinian people, I decided to dedicate myself primarily to helping Palestinians cope with Israeli oppression. As a result of this decision, since 1967 I have witnessed the daily injustices against Palestinians that most Israeli Jews preferred to overlook. My continual representing of Palestinians in Israeli courts angered most of my compatriots. Some perceived me as a pariah, others as an enemy of the people; cynics said I was on the payroll of the PLO. After the devastating Israeli invasion in Lebanon, and now, with the Palestinian uprising dominating the scene, quite a few left-wing Israelis and others have begun to view differently my years of pursuing justice. They are beginning to realize that maybe all these years I was working for a more humane, more just, more fair Israeli society. They are beginning to admit that for years they were myopic as to the gross injustices and the trampling of human rights that resulted from Israeli oppression. Yes, these Israelis are beginning to sense that my work over the years often served as a bridge for Israeli-Palestinian dialogue.

So my belief in dialogue was a result of my pursuit of justice, which for me is—well, let me say it—a passion. Do not misunderstand me, I am not a fanatic. I believe in democracy, in political pluralism, in the need for strong and fair judicial structures. Gross injustice sickens me to the marrow of my bones; ruthless infliction of suffering is something I cannot physically ignore.

Let me give two general examples of how justice is daily distorted in Israel. (I will end this article with a more detailed specific example.) One need not go to the courts to see this distortion; a sensitive person need only open the newspaper and read about what is happening. The first example has to do with the Israeli military courts in the occupied territories, which have become tribunals that usually ride roughshod over the pursuit of justice. Lately I reached a decision to stop appearing in these courts in order to represent Palestinians. My main reason for this decision is that these courts are all geared toward organizing plea-bargaining deals with accused Palestinians. By being "geared" I mean that the defendant is warned that if he or she will plea bargain, he or she will be let off with a mild sentence; but if one does not plea bargain, one will continue to be interrogated, and at times physically tortured, and will finally be sentenced to a much greater punishment. Quite a few innocent Palestinians choose to plead guilty and to plea bargain rather than undergo continual torture and risk the danger of a long sentence. The judges know that this is occurring. For me this method has become a travesty of justice. I refuse to play the game according to these rules.

Second, I have repeatedly warned my compatriots that in Israel we are becoming used to three standards of justice and systems of judicial inquiry. There is a standard of justice and a system of judicial inquiry for Jews whose views accord with the national consensus. There is another system and standard for Arabs who are Israeli citizens. The Palestinians in the occupied territories are ruled by so-called military justice. And a third system and standard exists for Jews whose views do not accord with the national consensus. Let me add that the daily exploitation and oppression of Palestinians by Jewish settlers in the occupied territories is in accord with the national consensus, while the criticizing of such deeds is called antipatriotic. I rebel against this triple standard and system, and I speak out against it.

In my life the passion for justice daily blends with compassion. I feel the suffering of the Palestinians who live under military rule and who want to live in freedom and dignity. And why should they not aspire to freedom? This compassion is probably

why (although I have never agreed to represent in court a Palestinian who deliberately killed civilians) I never ask a person
whom I do represent what are his or her political convictions.
They are irrelevant to one's suffering, to one's plight, to the
details of one's accusation. Thus although I know that compassion need not lead to dialogue, in my case it often did, because
I always accept each Palestinian whom I represent as a whole
being, with his or her political convictions, and such acceptance
is central to the dialogical relationship.

Looking back on these years of struggle I am struck by the
fact that the pursuit of justice and the quest for dialogue are
often lonely endeavors. At times, when I speak in court about
the sufferings of a Palestinian suspect, or about a gross injustice
sanctioned by the court, I seem to hear only the echo of my own
voice. As my books show, I have been exposed to this loneliness
in court again and again and again, although judges and pros-
ecutors have at times praised the eloquence of my pleadings and
the profundity of my arguments. Thus with my books. Very few
Israelis want to read them, to learn about the incidents that I
describe, to perhaps rethink their political commitments and
beliefs. Put bluntly, even many intelligent persons among my
fellow Jews refuse to acknowledge the fact that Jews can per-
form and are performing evil deeds.

I am also responsible for my existential situation. The past
twenty-two years of my life have been a long mission, perhaps
an impossible mission. And when a person, and especially a
woman, is committed to such a mission, she will have little time
for establishing friendships. Always the next case is calling,
always a new instance of injustice is racking one's mind, the
witnessing of uncalled for brutality and suffering is once again
making one break into a cold sweat. Add to these exigencies
that I am committed to documenting the facts, to publishing
them, and that such documenting and writing is also often a
lonely endeavor. Thus moments of genuine dialogue often came
as a chance encounter during my self-imposed extended mission.
And yet, I want to speak out for dialogue because that is one
of the most important ways to emerge from the quagmire of evil
into which we Israelis are slowly but steadily sinking. But before

turning to dialogue, maybe here is the place to speak of betrayals.

What has happened in Israel is that all the key concepts have been betrayed by the leaders. And this betrayal has been accepted by the masses, many of whom chose to be cheated and to be misled by official propaganda. The problem is not only that these masses placidly accepted Ariel Sharon's brutal and bloody misadventure in Lebanon in 1982 or Yitzchak Rabin's inhumane and ruthless iron-fist policy against the Palestinians since 1988. I want to state categorically that Rabin is the most cruel defense minister we have had during the twenty-three years of the occupation of Palestinian lands. The problem is that all our basic concepts have become lies, lies that have struck roots deep in our everyday existence. Take the fact that the Labor Party, which calls itself a socialist party and sends its representatives to actively participate in every international socialist forum, has been pursuing and supporting a ruthless colonialist policy, which has exploited workers on the West Bank and the Gaza Strip since 1967. According to this policy the fate of most of the residents of these occupied areas under Israeli rule was to be the underpaid day laborers of an affluent capitalistic Israeli economy. And the daily implementation of this policy was pursued while the party boldly waved the banner of socialism.

Or take the fact that at least part of the right-wing Likud party calls itself "liberal" and this party has for years been denying civil and political rights to the Palestinian people as a matter of principle. Such a denial is spelled out in the party's political platform. Yet these so-called liberals duly participate in international forums that discuss the importance of civil and political rights. Or take the manner in which some religious Jews are utilizing and manipulating Judaism to justify brutality against Palestinians, to applaud the robbing of their land—as if these neighbors of ours were not also created by the God in whom they believe. Such gross betrayals, supported by bad faith and self-deceit, surround us everywhere.

Here is an example of how we betray concepts, which I wrote about in my latest book. It has to do with a catch phrase that has become popular in Israel when discussing Israeli soldiers: "they shoot and then cry":

> In a literal sense this [catch phrase] was true. After all, you can't cry when you're squinting down the barrel of a rifle. But I realized that as they were shooting, and then weeping, these gunmen had fallen in love with the nobility of their actions. Those who overheard the sobbing proclaimed that only in this country can you find young men of such character, who pity the fallen enemy, who share in the pain. These are purifying and protective tears, no one is as sensitive as we are, no one as gentle and as pure hearted. Tears and feelings—for many people they act as a sedative for conscience....
>
> Their hypocrisy crushes my heart because I know the dark side of their moon, the truth of what our soldiers did in Lebanon, and the true face of the occupation.[2]

I have been trying to show that our milieu nurtures the betrayal of concepts, even personal concepts such as the shedding of tears. Needless to say, in such a milieu only a few acknowledge the significance of dialogue—perhaps because genuine dialogue requires cleansing words from their deceitful usage, from their being manipulated by power-hungry politicians and promoters of mendacity. At times I feel that there are so many betrayals of the basic concepts of our political and personal life that we seem to be existing in some sort of haze, or thick, mountain fog, and that we cannot see beyond the next few steps. I am not suggesting that dialogue can cure all of that, but it is a constructive way to begin to seek truth and justice for our two peoples. It is also a way to rescue our souls from succumbing to the surrounding evil.

But there is a vicious circle here. For dialogue to occur, we must be willing to call a spade a spade. Military occupation is military occupation and not the freeing of land. (In general, freedom is a concept that applies to persons, not to innate objects.) The Palestinian uprising is a popular uprising and not organized disruptions of public order. Oppressing political rights is oppression, and not a security measure. And killing is killing, whether the soldier sheds tears afterward or not. Unfortunately, such truthfulness is what we Israelis have learned to evade.

Thus, I believe that my activity has been pursued in the spirit of dialogue.

Again and again I have confronted my fellow Israelis and called a spade a spade. I have listened to their responses, and even if those were cruel and brutal responses, I have tried to explain forcefully why I believe they are wrong. And I have also spoken dialogically to Palestinians, explaining to them that, despite the many injustices they suffer under the Israeli occupation, the only solution is peace with their Israeli neighbors by establishing a Palestinian state alongside Israel and not instead of it. I said this, together with other supporters of freedom for the Palestinians, to leaders of the PLO already in 1976, when they were totally against the idea of two states for two peoples; in that period they called for a secular democratic state in all of Palestine. I said it then, and they listened. Their present conciliatory policy, which is an advantage for all of us, may have been partially influenced by those dialogues. I have learned from such dialogical experiences that despite the callous responses that I may at times be subject to, many persons do listen. They want to hear what a person like myself is saying, even if they will later strive to dismiss my ideas from their mind.

Perhaps my strength in speaking dialogically arises from the fact that I am doing with my life what I fully believe is worthy of being done — in my case it is the pursuing of justice, the alleviating of undue suffering. Thus there is a mellowing joy that accompanies my frustrations and failures, a joy in my being able to engage my physical and mental powers in order to struggle for justice, and to do it by attempting to convince other people. And I struggle to convince these people not only by legal or rational arguments. I primarily attempt to convince by giving my whole being, which includes my belief in justice, to the person with whom I am conversing.

Probably the best way to close this rather abstract personal testimony is by giving a living example of one of my struggles. Let me briefly describe some highlights of the case of Ibrahim

Yasser Mohammad Al-Mator, which was recently closed by the Israel Supreme Court. As lawyer for the family I firmly believe that justice was obstructed, and I wrote a summary of my views. Here are some excerpts.

On July 8, 1988, the late Ibrahim Al-Mator was arrested by the Israeli security forces and brought to Dahariya detention camp, called "Dvir." Two months later he was transferred to the detention center called "Ofer." He was charged with security offenses at the military court in Ramallah. As far as the family knows, he denied the charges. The last court session in his trial was held on October 12, 1988; he was brought to the military court in Ramallah from Ofer. The family was present in court and noted that he was in good health; the continuation of the trial was set for November 9, 1988. His wife and his cousin visited him on the following day, October 13, and noted that his physical and mental health were satisfactory.

The following information about Al-Mator's last days was given to the family by released detainees.

Al-Mator was working in the kitchen at Ofer at the time the detainees there held a hunger strike in response to the harsh conditions of detention. The prison administration accused Al-Mator of organizing the strike, since he was known as a person who stood firm against the administration in the prisoners' struggle for bettering their conditions. There is also a testimony that Al-Mator exposed thefts of food from the kitchen (by the prison authorities?) and therefore was forbidden to work in the kitchen.

One of the detainees at Ofer told the family that after roll call on October 18, 1988, at 9:00 A.M., Al-Mator was taken from the center of the line and returned only at 11:30 A.M. Sand was seen on his shirt, trousers, and hair. He took his clothes and said that he was being transferred, but he did not know his destination. When they handcuffed him near the bus and forcefully put him on it, he managed to shout: "They're demanding that I work with them, but I'm clean, just know that." He was then forcefully silenced.

Al-Mator was brought to Dahariya in a bus, alone, on October 18 at around 4:00 P.M. and the detainees saw him taken off the vehicle with blood flowing from his head, especially from behind his ear. Upon arriving Al-Mator shouted "Allah Akbar. I am Ibrahim Al-Mator, they are beating me to death, detainees, witness!" He was locked in a solitary cell and was not seen again, but his shouts were heard for two days. When they ceased, he was no longer among the living.

Indeed Al-Mator's silence indicated his death, and his body was given to his family for burial on October 21, 1988. The military authorities forced the family to hold a hurried funeral for the deceased. Based on the testimonies of relatives—Al-Mator's wife, grandfather, brothers, and sister—the following details emerged.

On the deceased's head there was congealed blood stuck to his hair. There were stitched wounds behind his ears, the stitching seemed to be piecing together wide tears in the skin, in different directions. His right arm seemed fractured in several places. On the wrists there were blue marks left by handcuffs. Similar blue marks were on the ankles. When the family tried to turn the body over in order to see Al-Mator's back, the soldiers forbade them to do so; during the attempt the two brothers saw bruises that were probably the results of beating on the deceased's back. When the deceased's uncle asked Captain Yehiya: "What did he do to you that you killed him?" the officer replied: "Anyone who starts up with us, his fate will be the same."

All the above evidence led the family to the conclusion that Al-Mator was murdered by IDF soldiers while he was in prison, and the version about his suicide was not true.

Al-Mator's family reached my office on October 25, 1988. On October 26, 1988, I sent a letter of complaint to the minister of defense, to the attorney general, and to the legal advisor of Judea and Samaria with a demand to investigate and to put those responsible for Al-Mator's death on trial for murder, to send me the autopsy report and the deceased's death certificate, and to order the opening of the deceased's grave in order to conduct an autopsy by a pathologist on behalf of the family without delay. I received no reply from any of the recipients of my letters.

A month later I appealed on behalf of the family to the Supreme Court of Israel. I will skip over the details of my appeal, the delaying tactics employed by the representative of the state of Israel, and the final decision by the Supreme Court to open the grave and reexamine the body. I only want to mention two important details that emerged in this period.

First, in the autopsy report, which I finally received on December 8, 1988, there was only one sentence about the circumstances of the death of Al-Mator: "On October 21, 1988, [Al-Mator] was found hanging in a detention cell in Hebron." There is not one more word about the circumstances of the death, the manner of the hanging, the implements used, the size of the cell, or any other details.

The importance of such detail was stressed by Dr. Robert Kirschner, a pathologist and expert in forensic medicine from Chicago, who is also a member of Physicians for Human Rights. I wrote to Dr. Kirschner and sent him the autopsy report. After carefully reviewing the autopsy report, Dr. Kirschner wrote:

> An autopsy conducted according to all proper regulations of forensic medicine concerning a victim who died as the result of strangulation demands that the noose by means of which the deceased is said to have been hung be presented to the pathologist in order to determine if its shape suits the shape of injury on the neck. Here we have no evidence that the noose was examined at all by the pathologist. In which cell had the victim been, was there a place in it where he could have tied the noose? Had he been bound while in the cell? Who "discovered" him and who else was in the area? Abrasions and signs of injury are evidence enough that the deceased had been beaten, but conducting incisions in the joints during the autopsy could have shown additional injuries.

The second detail has to do with the investigation of Al-Mator's death as conducted by the investigating military police. They asked me to help them summon Palestinian witnesses who had reported to the family what had happened to Al-Mator in his last days. But the witnesses feared to be identified. Learning from previous instances in which Palestinians who had testified against Israeli cruelties had themselves been jailed and tortured, they refused to believe the guarantees given by representatives of the state.

When I pressed some of these witnesses, they answered something like the following:

> How can you guarantee that no harm will be done to me if I testify, when we are at the mercy of any soldier? You know that I can be placed under administrative detention without any charge, on the basis of secret material, which you will never be allowed to see. You know that I can be arrested and beaten for a thousand reasons, or even shot for no reason at all, and then you will be told that I tried to escape or that I attacked a soldier. Your guarantee is worthless in these circumstances.

Thus, no witness agreed to testify directly.

The investigation by the investigating military police revealed a few significant facts about the hours before Al-Mator's death, which I shall merely list. Al-Mator had been on a hunger strike. He had been sprayed with tear gas. He had been injected with Valium by the doctor under orders from the commander of the prison. He had been given painkillers. He had committed suicide during the forty-five minutes he was not seen by prison guards. His hands were handcuffed and his feet were shackled during this entire period.

Al-Mator's body was examined again in the presence of Professor Derek Pounder of Dundee, Scotland, the representative of Physicians for Human Rights. I will not go into the many details of his report, which revealed basic flaws in the previous autopsy made by Israeli authorities. He definitely stated that one cannot exclude the possibility that Al-Mator was murdered, or committed suicide as a desperate choice between continual torture and unbearable suffering or death. Professor Pounder also noted that the injection of Valium to the deceased by the prison doctor who was ordered to do so by the prison commander is an action that appears to constitute a breach of medical ethics.

I should like to emphasize once again that according to the report Al-Mator was handcuffed and his feet were shackled when he allegedly hung himself with a noose he had made from a strip torn from a blanket. He did this in the forty-five minutes when he was not seen by the prison guard. On the basis of all this evidence, I filed a request in the Israel Supreme Court for a new investigation of Al-Mator's death conducted by an impartial committee. Again, I will skip the details of the court discussion. Enough to point out that when I asked to see the noose, or the blanket from which the noose had been torn, the representative of the state replied that the noose had not been found, and the blanket from which the noose had been torn had disappeared.

All these details did not convince the Supreme Court. They decided that the investigation had been proper and closed the case. I was shocked, angry, frustrated.

I can only summarize: the death of Ibrahim Al-Mator, which occurred in an empty and isolated cell where he was alone with his shackles and blanket, when he was bound hand and foot, beaten and wounded, on hunger strike, sprayed with tear gas and injected with Valium, fed with painkillers the nature of which no one knows, screaming "I want to die" and finding no one to rescue him, hanged on a noose that cannot be found, made from a blanket that disappeared, did not arouse the judges of Israel's Supreme Court to order a new investigation.

Clearly justice was not done!

NOTES

1. Felicia Langer, *An Age of Stone* (London: Quartet Books, 1988).
2. Ibid., p. 146. The catch phrase later became a song. The Israeli government then duly decided that neither television nor radio could broadcast the song, which might intimate that the Palestinians are not totally to blame.

6

The Bridge of Dialogue:
Between Independent States

ZIAD ABU ZAYAD

At times I wonder as to the significance of distances. Here I, a Palestinian, have been living a few miles from Jews and Israelis for all my life—and yet I feel that there is still a great distance between many Jews and myself. At times I fear that for many of them, this distance is unbridgeable.

We are fated to live in this area of the world together, as neighbors. I reside in Eizariyeh, a village near Jerusalem. My family has lived here for more than five hundred years. After the Israeli occupation, part of my village was included in Jerusalem. The other section—where I live—is considered "West Bank," and is thus under Israeli military administration, with what such administration implies. Israelis call Jerusalem "The United Jerusalem." This city, which is holy to the monotheistic faiths, is only physically united. Jews and Arabs reside not far from each other, but exist at a great distance from each other.

My belief in dialogue grew during the many years I worked as a journalist. My career in journalism started as a hobby in 1969, while I was still practicing law. One of the areas in which I specialized was translating from the Hebrew press. In 1977 I was offered the post of senior editor for Israeli affairs with another Palestinian paper. One of my responsibilities was an entire page that included articles from the Israeli press, in which I tried to show that there were Israelis who rejected the occupation and their government policy, which denies us our freedom. I also included articles by right-wing Israelis so that our readers would be acquainted with the ideas of their oppressors, with the antidialogical sectors of Israeli society. I later became editor-in-chief of that newspaper, until I had a basic disagreement over policy with the publisher and was fired.

The idea that I, a Palestinian, put out a newspaper in Hebrew, *Gesher*, emerged by chance. After my being fired as the editor-in-chief of a major Arab daily newspaper, I went back to work as a lawyer. But after two years of sitting in an office and studying laws that dealt with my clients' cases, I felt hemmed in. I did not always like to wear a suit and tie, when as a journalist and editor I could walk around in a sportshirt and jeans. I felt the itch to write journalism and decided to find some way to return to the field.

I then said to myself, since everyone associates you with Palestinian-Israeli dialogue, why not put out a newspaper dedicated to dialogue. The result was *Gesher*, a Palestinian newspaper in Hebrew. I still make my living from my work as a lawyer, but through my work on *Gesher* I have not lost contact with journalism. It is a small, modest newspaper appearing once every two weeks and sold mainly to a few hundred subscribers. My lawyer's office is also the editorial office; my secretary also deals with editorial affairs. I decided to dedicate all the funds I earned from my lectures—between $100 and $150 per lecture—to supporting this newspaper. And these funds help keep *Gesher* alive. Unfortunately, I do not have enough funds to promote *Gesher*, so I suspect that quite a few interested Israelis have not yet heard of it.

Gesher is a newspaper of commentaries and of bringing the Palestinian approach to Israelis. It is not a newspaper that reports on daily developments in the area, although there are summary reports of important developments. To acquaint Israelis with some of the spiritual aspects of Palestinian life, I also include two pages dedicated to developments in literature and the arts in the Palestinian community. Today *Gesher* is a modest dialogical response to what I see as the constant brainwashing of Israelis by the government media.

The first Israeli I ever met was a soldier, a few hours after the cease fire in June 1967. I looked at him and was scared; I felt hatred burning in his eyes. Our encounter passed slowly but ended peacefully. He did not look at my face, but spoke with composure to the Greek Orthodox monk who accompanied me from the shelter in his church to my nearby home.

A few days later I met a second Israeli. An Israeli reserve soldier passed by my house and suddenly called out to my father, who was standing in the garden. They exchanged a few words and then shook hands warmly. They had been old friends who had worked together before 1948 in the municipality of Jerusalem. They renewed their friendship. After a couple of days this Israeli friend visited us at home and asked if we needed food. We declined, but we appreciated his offer. When borders between the occupied territories and Israel were opened, we met a few times and continued our acquaintance.

One decision I made soon after that was to learn Hebrew. I enrolled in an ulpan. It turned out to be an important decision for a person who believes in dialogue, since I soon learned that not all Israelis speak English. At the ulpan I also became acquainted with Israelis, and in August 1967 a Palestinian friend and I participated in a debate with Israeli counterparts in front of a large group of foreign students in the house of the Anglican bishop in Jerusalem.

I now recognize that my learning Hebrew was of utmost importance in helping me relate to Israelis. I met face to face with the entire spectrum of Israeli views, from right-wing fanatics to leftist Latin American emigrants. I developed greater sensitivity to the ideas and arguments of the different Israeli positions. Knowing that it was necessary to practice the language, I even helped a friend in the Old City of Jerusalem sell toys to Israelis who flooded the Arab sections of this city shortly after August 1967 in search of a bargain. I encouraged Israelis to visit friends who wished to host them.

My discussions with Israelis were generally cordial as long as we did not discuss politics. When we did discuss politics, the discussion usually became heated, with tensions on both sides. I usually tried to smooth over our differences, partially because I did not want to cut the newly forged links and relations, and also because, personally, I try to evade confrontations and tend to seek compromise.

My knowledge of Hebrew led to my being invited to speak to Israelis. This occurred through a friend who was arranging cultural evenings for kibbutzim. I started these lectures as fun, but I soon became known; over the years I continued to speak in kibbutzim and also to other audiences. I spoke about the Palestinian people and about our need for a state of our own. But I came to these lectures not only to explain and to teach, but also to listen and to learn. I learned about the Israelis' reservations and fears of Arab hostility; I also learned to recognize their empty rhetoric and to appreciate the moments of truth, when such emerged. At times I thought that such meetings were an exercise in futility, as when I was invited to lecture to thirty-five officers of the Israel Security Service who are active in ensuring the continuation of Israeli rule in the occupied territories. That was a ludicrous experience. When my host wanted to introduce me, one of them said, "We know Ziad Abu Zayad." I immediately responded, "I'm sure you've studied my file in your archives as preparation for this meeting." They laughed and tried to explain that they had seen me on television. Perhaps, but they also knew about me from their daily work.

In my lecturing over the years I learned to appreciate persons who wanted to relate dialogically. They were not many. For some kibbutz members, lectures were a manner of entertaining themselves. They came to argue, not to discuss or to learn. Lately, with the polarization in Israeli society, I have become more selective in responding to invitations to lecture. I will not accept an invitation to a meeting that will be dedicated to arguing and bickering, instead of to listening and learning from each other, like some meetings with elder members of kibbutzim. But yet I welcome meetings with Israeli youth before military service and with students.

The distances exist. Mainly in our minds. For instance, I am again and again surprised how misinformed the Israeli population is as to our beliefs and political stance. I can only conclude that some of the Israeli media participate in brainwashing the public about Palestinian views. Many Israelis are totally blind to developments in the Palestinian political stance; they do not want to listen to our suggestions about how to resolve our differences. They still argue that the Palestinians want to evacuate the Jews from the "land of Israel" and to set up a state from the Jordan to the Mediterranean. Many of them do not see that the decision to recognize Israel accepted by the Palestinian National Council was the culmination of a process that began two decades previously. Of course, we Palestinians who years ago advocated dialogue with Israel were then abused by our people. But slowly we succeeded in convincing the majority of the Palestinian people led by the PLO that mutual recognition and dialogue is the way to reach peace, and that we can live as a nation on a section of historical Palestine.

What gravely disturbs me is that the Israeli establishment, most of the Israeli media, and a large portion of the Israeli people ignore these developments toward dialogue and peace with Israel within the Palestinian people and its representatives, namely the PLO. Somehow I feel that the myth of the Palestinian enemy is something that many Israelis refuse to relinquish. They seem to wish that the distance between us remain unsurpassable; in other words, they refuse to recognize our freedom. To buttress their isolationist approach, they cite statements by extreme splinter groups within the Palestinian people, groups that call for the annihilation of Israel. But much as Israel has its extremists, we have our radicals.

My general impression is that many Israelis and many Palestinians are prodialogue. But I also sense that there are many more Israelis than Palestinians who are vehemently antidialogue. These antidialogical people refuse to meet with Palestinians and to speak with them. They regard themselves as too good to speak straightforwardly with an Arab. For instance, in the summer of 1989, together with a Jewish lawyer, I went to a prison camp to visit one of my clients. After waiting about two hours for permission to see our clients, we both complained to a major in charge of the camp. But he refused to look at me and to speak in my direction. He only responded to the Jewish lawyer, as if I did not exist, as if I was not standing two feet from him.

In my dialogue with persons from the Israeli left, I criticize them on two important matters. First, they attempt to blame us Palestinians for their failure to convince their fellow Israelis to support their views. Every so often a few of us get a call and an Israeli whom we greatly respect tells us that if we were to come out with a certain proclamation, it would enhance the power of the Israeli left. Now the interesting thing about such an argument is that it has almost no validity.

For instance, before the Palestinian National Council (PNC) decided to accept U.N. resolutions 181, 242, and 338, which guarantee Israel's right to exist and its security, we were told by many persons associated with what is called the Israeli Peace Camp, that if only Yasir Arafat would accept these resolutions, it would give much support to their arguments. Some of them even believed that it would bring a basic change—a few even said a revolutionary change—in the attitudes of most Israelis. Unfortunately, that belief of the Israeli Peace Camp turned out to be false. U.N. resolutions 181, 242, and 338 were accepted by the PNC more than a year ago and did not convince most of the Israelis that we want peace. But the Israeli left did not learn from this episode and continues to demand that we come out with statements that will strengthen them. I can only add that the problem of the Israeli left is to convince their fellow Israelis that our demands are just, and that the Israeli government must enter into dialogue with our representatives. From my experience, our proclamations have very little influence on this internal discussion.

My second criticism of the Israeli Peace Camp is that it is splintered into small groups, and that there are many groups unwilling to work together. Often these groups do not understand that we are confronted by a grave political problem, and in order to confront it successfully they must learn to work together. I do not mean that they should deny their differences, but rather that they should learn to dialogue with each other in order to create a united front that will work courageously together for peace.

Personally, my quest for dialogue has led to many close relations with Israelis. We do not always agree, at times we disagree vehemently, but the basic accepting of the other person with his or her otherness continues to sustain our relationships. This has been a most gratifying experience. Once I was jailed for what in any country would be merely a misdemeanor. I drove a car with an Israeli yellow license plate, while we Palestinians are allowed to drive a car only with a blue license plate, which indicates that the driver is from the occupied territories. The reason I drove that car was that I had purchased it from an Israeli and I wanted to bring it home where I could arrange for the correct license plate to be put on. I was caught and immediately jailed for eighteen days, which is the maximum time a Palestinian can be jailed without being brought before a judge. My Israeli friends intervened and picketed outside the police station where I was held. They argued with the commander of the station; they aroused the media. Thanks to them I was released after six days.

These friends have been supportive over the years. Such friendships encourage me to believe that distances can be bridged.

With all my belief in the importance of dialogue as a way of life, I must admit that now, in the historical situation we Palestinians find ourselves, I feel that I must be practical. My people, we Palestinians, are daily oppressed by the Israeli army, and one of my major goals in entering dialogue with Israelis should be to encourage them to stop the oppression. That is why we must direct our attempts at dialogue to people who can make a difference in Israel, to political leaders of parties that have some power.

We must understand that today our basic problem, the problem of attaining freedom, is a political problem. Each person who has the craving for freedom must strive to bring about political change. This is a change in the political relations between the Israeli nation and the Palestinian nation. We want a peaceful political change, we aspire to attain peace and freedom. We are willing to attain these goals through dialogue. But, as it looks now, we will attain these goals only through a long, arduous political struggle, which will probably include civil disobedience and at times minor violence.

Furthermore, we have internal problems to which we must also attend. For instance, we have to convince our people that we must not export the uprising, we must not commit violence within Israel, or against Jews in Europe or the United States. Ours must be a struggle for freedom in our limited land. Stabbing an Israeli in the streets of Tel Aviv does not help our struggle, nor does it convince the Israelis or world opinion that we are struggling for our freedom. On the contrary, it will cause our struggle great damage in the Israeli public opinion. Convincing our people of these views is difficult because the Israeli forces use extreme violence and oppression against our unarmed civilians and thus push them toward violent reactions. Furthermore Israeli authorities gravely limit our possibilities of meeting and of discussing political issues. In short, we have a problem with our radicals and fanatics, much as the Israelis have problems with their radicals and fanatics. I fear that a long period of oppression and occupation can create a breeding ground for such antidialogical forces and for a deepening of hatred and hostility.

Let me close this rather personal testimony with my dream of how I would like to see this area in ten years. I would like to see two independent states, Israel and Palestine, with open borders, with a mutual concern for the future of the land, the air, and the water of the area, with a wish to learn from each other's tradition, culture, and social and scientific achievements. I dream of a Palestinian state that needs no army and no military-industrial complex, because it lives at peace with its neighbors. I dream of Jerusalem being an open united city where the overall municipality is shared by Jews and Arabs, while each community governs its section of the city, and each person in the city respects persons of other nations and persons who believe in the other monotheistic faiths. In short, I dream of the distances between us being bridged by genuine dialogue.

And personally, I dream of the day I will leave my home in the morning and know that I will return for sure in the evening, without being arrested for expressing my thoughts. I also dream of going to sleep at night and being sure that I will wake up in the morning in my own home, without being harassed or picked up by a nightly visit of the Israel Security Service.

SECTION 4

DIALOGUE AND EDUCATION

Probably the saddest aspect of the continual strife between Israelis and Palestinians is that within the educational systems there is no emphasis on the need for dialogue and for mutual respect. We said the situation is sad; perhaps a better word would be surrealistic. Eighty Palestinian school-age children under the age of sixteen were killed by Israeli soldiers in the second year of the *intifada*. Twenty-eight of these were children under the age of twelve. But the horror of these killings has not penetrated the school system in Israel. Children in Israel continue to learn that Judaism values human life, that even on Yom Kippur one must value human life before prayer or fasting. But this valuing is not linked to the current situation in Israel-Palestine. Surrealistic? Yes, but also deceitful. Our children are implicitly taught that the corpses of killed Palestinian children should *quietly* rot in their graves, because we Jews know how to respect human life.

Much of this deceit and surrealism begins at the university level. These supposed free havens of thought in Israel seem to be spiritually bankrupt, if by spirituality one means responding, in the spirit of the Hebrew prophets, to the unjust situation at hand. Few, very few, professors have dared to speak out forcefully against the persecution, oppression, and exploitation of Palestinians. Here and there a professor may softly recommend a more humane approach toward Palestinians. Like Dante in his visit to the inferno, these soft-spoken academicians seem merely to be weeping in their souls at the atrocities and sufferings that their eyes behold.

Israeli students are not better. For almost three years the Palestinian universities in the occupied territories have been virtually closed by decision of the Israeli military. Thousands of Palestinian students have not been able to complete their studies. Not once during these three years has the Israeli student association attempted to assist these Palestinian students or to find ways of relating dialogically to them. Indifference to the Palestinian students' plight reigns unmolested among their Israeli counterparts.

Thus the hidden and not so hidden curriculum in Israeli universities is antidialogical, and with that very antispiritual. Here, we submit, we accept Martin Buber's criterion: where the quest for dialogue is despised, spirituality evaporates. This situation is most unfortunate because the coming generation of teachers and leaders is now passing through the Israeli universities, and they are learning well the lessons of this hidden curriculum. They are learning to be betrayers of their Jewish heritage, because by sanctioning antidialogical approaches the professors and students in Israeli universities today are betraying their spiritual heritage.

Hanan Mikhail-Ashrawi teaches English at Birzeit University on the West Bank. Haim Gordon teaches philosophy of education at Ben Gurion University of the Negev in Beer Sheva. Although they both have been involved in promoting Israeli-Palestinian dialogue for years, they have approached the promotion of dialogue from different directions. While Mikhail-Ashrawi has been working for Israeli-Palestinian dialogue on the political and international level, Gordon has been working for such dialogue at the grassroots level. The difference in their respective approaches is well felt in their essays.

Despite this difference, and despite the difference of style, the essays are united not only in the quest for dialogue. They also both confront the evil approaches that result from the antidialogical stance of the current Israeli government under Prime Minister Yitzchak Shamir. This willingness to confront evil from within the academic community is rare in Israel, and we suspect in many academic communities in the world. Our impression is that academicians want to analyze, to understand, to observe, to discuss, to write up—they hate to confront evil. But the non-confronting of evil allows it to continue to exist. Hanan Mikhail-Ashrawi and Haim Gordon are willing to confront evil while struggling for dialogue. This willingness adds originality and courage to their quest for dialogue.

7

Principles, Politics, and Pronouns: Evolution of the Palestinian-Israeli Dialogue

HANAN MIKHAIL-ASHRAWI

In the context of the Palestinian-Israeli conflict and the evolution of its conceptual and political discourse, the term "dialogue" has undergone a complex semiotic transformation and accrual of significance in direct relation to its specific or concrete political environment or event. Starting with definition by negation, nondialogue dominated Palestinian-Israeli discourse for a long time as an affirmation of conflict and the non-recognition by either side of the other in a mutually exclusive equation, whereby any direct verbal "contact" was perceived as an implicit admission of existence, hence legitimacy. Moreover, the absence of dialogue served as an active instrument of hostility and denial characterized by the hurling of semantic missiles *at* each other (rather than *to* each other) through the use of an intermediary who served the function of being the ostensible addressee, or the object that served to deflect these missiles to their real target. At this stage, nondialogue was indirectly confrontational, preceding even the stage of "hostile dialogue," which addresses the adversary directly albeit in a noncommunicative and blind exchange of ossified linguistic (hence behavioral) constructs. The use of the first- and third-person pronoun rather than the first- and second-person, which is essential to dialogue, dominated the nondialogue stage and allowed for excesses, distortions, and misdirections, which the apparent target felt under no compunction to counter or redress, being part of the tacit understanding that the real target lay elsewhere.

Contemporary political realities, however, have imposed new imperatives, which necessitated the forging of new tools of discourse while rendering the "we-they" paradigm ineffective and obsolete. The Palestinian *intifada*, as an assertion of the collective popular will, has imbued Palestinian discourse with legitimacy and authenticity, stemming from the actual confrontation between military might and the human will to resist, between subjugation by force and the determination not to submit, between occupier and occupied, and consequently has restored some equilibrium to an inherently asymmetrical condition by injecting the weight of moral ascendancy into the scale in favor of the victim, while simultaneously stripping the oppressor of the traditional advantages of physical and verbal domination. When, in November 1988, the Palestine National Council articulated the Palestinian political program and launched its peace offensive, much of its motivation and legitimacy was due, in fact, to this restorative aspect of the *intifada* — that is not to underestimate the natural progression and evolution of Palestinian political perceptions and discourse, which came as a result of the cumulative experience of the struggle for national liberation — most significantly in the camps of Lebanon. However, as a phase of condensation and acceleration in this progression, the *intifada* has rendered peace discourse inevitable. At the heart of this discourse lies the complex, problematic, and often amorphous concept of dialogue.

During the nondialogue stage, although Israel maintained a public prodialogue stance, it was clear to Palestinians that this stance was not a genuine drive toward communication as conflict-resolution leading to reconciliation, but rather as a perpetuation and reenforcement of Israeli aggression and control extending from the military to the physical/demographic to the verbal/propagandistic to the perceptual, and finally to the political level. From the Palestinian perspective, the predialogue actual and potential points of contact then had a six-tier manifestation:

1. *Personal-political* cooperation of limited scope and frequency, but taking place between and among like-minded Palestinians and Israelis who share a common political perspective or ideology.

2. *Personal-exploitive*, which manifested itself mainly in the unequal labor relations of employer vs. employee as another form of domination and exploitation often characterized by racism and discrimination (on both class and national grounds), further enhancing hostility and resentment, and gradually preparing for the next step.

3. *Collective-exploitive* situation as a result of the growth of an increasingly alienated and oppressed Palestinian working class; in addition, the underlying economic basis of such exploitation found expression in the strangulation of any real or possible Palestinian economic independence or growth as a means of transforming the whole population into a captive consumer society as an outlet and a guaranteed market for Israeli products and produce.

4. *Personal-asymmetrical*, superficial attempts at normalizing relations through social or economic contacts to serve the self-interest of both sides whereby the inequality and disequilibrium were willfully ignored for the sake of personal gain, but primarily serving to create an artificial "normalcy" in the midst of an inherently "abnormal" condition of occupation—short-lived and perceived as futile attempts at "defusing" conflict.

5. *Collective-national* as the most obvious and prevalent form of contact between the Israeli army and institutions of occupation on the one hand, and the whole civilian Palestinian population under occupation on the other—in all cases serving the interests of the former in exercising direct control over the latter, whether through military violence or institutionalized coercion ("civil administration" offices, intelligence activities, etc.) or expressing the will of the latter to reject and resist the domination of the former (demonstrations, strikes, boycott, etc.).

6. *Collective-political* dialogue between legitimate represen-

tatives of both parties, which remained nonexistent despite Israeli attempts at creating "alternative" leadership from among the Palestinians under occupation to circumvent or replace the PLO as the legitimate leadership and interlocuters of all Palestinians, or at establishing quisling groups (such as the Village Leagues) to usurp this legitimacy; this led to the further undermining of any genuine dialogue through misdirection and negation.

The emergence of real dialogue possibilities following the Palestinian peace initiative has by no means entirely eliminated the above points of contact, but has rather served to shift emphasis and to create additional avenues for positive contact. The options have become possible primarily through the dual and mutually dependent legitimacies of the *intifada* as the human substance and moral force of the political agenda and the PLO as the genuine articulator of the peace initiative and the interlocutor on behalf of all the Palestinian people. It is misleading, however, to assume that the admissibility of a Palestinian-Israeli dialogue immediately following the Palestinian peace initiative (and even up to the present) has been unequivocal or unconditional. Many pitfalls and obstacles threaten to undermine or even entirely sabotage its progress, and these will be addressed in detail later. At this stage, it has become apparent that the tentative and exploratory attempts at dialogue have taken three basic channels or tributaries, which will ultimately converge into a holistic peace drive:

1. Grassroots or unofficial popular dialogue through joint action groups. The ground work for much of this coordination was prepared by the "personal-political" contacts and cooperation between primarily left-wing individuals and small groups from both sides who shared common principles and goals, dating back to the early 1970s. At that time it was "unfashionable" and often dangerous to form such connections or alliances, and many Israeli activists were subjected to the "Palestinian treatment" for daring to express their solidarity or principled agreement with Palestinians (a most notable example being the beating, tear-gassing, and detention of the Committee in Solidarity with Birzeit University). Though limited in number, their actions were primarily street-oriented with a clear political motivation

and perspective. The gradual growth of the Peace Camp, especially in the late 1980s, not only augmented their numbers but brought a new type of peace activist into the arena with a different political agenda and a variety of priorities, objectives, and tactics. As such, the marginalization of the earlier activists was seen as detrimental, and the newcomers sought to influence "mainstream" politics through political platforms and events that were not in danger of being labeled "extremist" or "disruptive," but that enjoyed a legitimacy within the established political structure and ideology. Palestinian contacts and dialogue expanded accordingly.

While continuing on questions of shared political principles and strategy with the traditional, often termed "historical," allies of the Palestinian cause, new relationships are being formed with the "peace activists" who are emerging as a quantitative (as well as qualitative) force from Israeli society as a whole. People-to-people contacts among specific sectors of both societies are being established with renewed vigor, especially among women (Coalition and Network Israeli women with Palestinian women's committees and independents), academics and other professionals, and students. All share a commitment to the peace process on the basis of the principles of mutuality, reciprocity, self-determination, and legitimacy. Most of their joint activities serve to increase political awareness, education, and mobilization toward this end, especially in Israeli society, whether through demonstrations, house meetings, public lectures and seminars, or mass events (e.g., the peace march and human chain of December 1989, or the women's rally of March 1990). Many of these contacts are enhanced and reinforced by the second type of dialogue, the international conference.

2. International conferences, or Palestinian-Israeli dialogue activities within an international framework. From Amsterdam to Prague to Paris to The Hague to London to New York to Brussels to Toledo to Milan, Palestinians and Israelis in search of peace carry their historical luggage and unfold the burden of their conflict for public perusal and resolution. Such dialogues take the forms of debate, argument, discussion, and sometimes mutual concurrence in a spirit ranging from historical recrimination and accusation through patronizing advice and defen-

siveness to relieved, though sometimes forced, amiability. Sensitivities and taboos are as often evaded as violated, but with each encounter a new level of candor and understanding is achieved in an incremental effect. The objectives and achievements of these conferences—as seen by hindsight—may be summed up as follows:

a. As public relations exercises, they have a tremendous impact on the public opinion of the host country and serve to motivate political forces and grassroot organizations for further action as a result of participation in and exposure to the particular dynamic of the dialogue.

b. Since no Palestinian from the occupied territories participates in any conference unless the PLO is visibly and officially represented, the occasion serves to underline the unity of the Palestinian people and to enhance the legitimacy of PLO leadership before Israeli and international public opinion.

c. In like manner, Israeli peace activists serve to introduce and "normalize" the PLO to their own public, while building bridges and relationships of significant political import.

d. Consequently, a mood of mutual understanding and "humanization" is generated with a momentum capable of leading to genuine negotiations without the distortions of suspicion, mistrust, and ignorance.

e. As confidence-building measures, these conferences also serve as simulations of real negotiations within the international conference, although the Israeli participants in particular are not representative.

f. They further increase each side's knowledge of the other, and specifically of those "thorny" issues or problematic areas that may hamper real negotiations, and thus allow each side to prepare for them in advance. Conversely, they gradually expand the domain of common agreement through cumulative effort and incremental achievement.

g. Finally, consciously or inadvertently, political positions and platforms undergo a process of modification and transformation on both sides to accommodate the experience and knowledge gained through such meetings. Understandably, each side attempts to influence the other while trying to maintain its own position. Such changes, however, are a double-edged sword and must be carefully evaluated.

In all these conferences, redundancy and overexposure can render their continuation counterproductive. At best, they must not be undertaken lightly. In all cases an evaluative pause is required to assess their achievements, delineate their pitfalls, and structure a future strategy for the accomplishment of specific objectives.

3. Secret, indirect, or "illegal" meetings between Israeli figures and the PLO. The most prominent examples of such meetings are those of Ezer Weisman and Abie Nathan with PLO personalities. They brought down the force of Israeli law on the two Israelis (in varying degrees) leading to punitive measures. Reports of other meetings, proximity talks, or secret communications are of sufficient frequency in the media as to render them probable and real. Their occurrence, especially among official or public figures, is of great significance as a form of pre-negotiation dialogue; however, the nature, substance, and accomplishments of these meetings must remain a task of the future, pending their full disclosure.

Before moving on to the last phase of the Palestinian-Israeli dialogue, which actually incorporates "dialogue" into the peace process as a concrete step, it is time to pause, ask a few questions, and attempt to reach some answers pertinent to the understanding and evaluation of the voluntary type of dialogue mentioned above. The questions may be summed up as follows: Is dialogue necessary? If so, then what are its objectives and accomplishments? What are its prerequisites? And finally, what are its pitfalls?

At this stage, the Palestinian peace initiative and the *intifada* have legitimized the principle of dialogue (as a first- and second-person discourse) by providing the political framework and the human substance of the dialogue. Among the justifications given for the sanctioning of the voluntary (and often structured) dialogue is mainly communication as a means of acquiring knowledge directly and dispelling preconceptions, stereotyping, and prejudice, thus replacing the stance of hostility and suspicion with one more conducive to conflict resolution on the basis of increased understanding and a disposition toward reconciliation. Admittedly, the process has to be gradual, though ultimately inseparable from the totality of measures grouped under the general heading, "confidence-building." As a prenegotiations phase, dialogue can effectively create a momentum for peace (a negotiated settlement) by preparing and disseminating the discourse and atmosphere most suitable and conducive to negotiations between the legitimate representatives of both peoples, the PLO and the Israeli government. The international dimension also brings into this dynamic the future role of the international community as part of the peace conference, which will provide settlement with legitimacy and guarantees.

In addition to the seven items discussed earlier (under "international conferences"), the purposes and objectives of all types of voluntary dialogue include the double achievement of bringing the occupation home to the Israelis as a reality they cannot afford to ignore, while providing the Palestinians with the opportunity to narrate, to present themselves directly, and to articulate their case in person and in their own words. As such, dialogue becomes a force of moral/humane substantiation, gradually leading to a process of mutual legitimization, which is essential for successful negotiations. Similarly, an incremental process of mutual authentication of political programs and agendas is an important preparatory stage for effective negotiations. More immediately and specifically, a mutual support system is created for mobilization and organization toward peace in the participants' respective communities, but mainly among Israelis who lack a peace consensus or majority. Among Palestinians, dialogue—especially in the form of grassroots or joint action groups—allows for the monitoring of human rights violations by the Israeli occupation authorities, and often develops into preventive action. All encounters, furthermore, are inseparable from their basic definition as popular empowerment, which will eventually be translated into official policy. Ultimately, Palestinians and Israelis share a historical responsibility as the two peoples who have to conclude peace together and are thus the parties most immediately and directly concerned. Consequently, they must work together to bring about a disengagement from the situation of conflict and disequilibrium (the occupation) in order to reengage on the basis of symmetry and equality.

Any attempt at engagement through dialogue must, by necessity, be carried out by individuals with a commitment to the success of the endeavor through both political awareness and personal predisposition. They must also enjoy a certain credibility and legitimacy within their respective communities if the dialogue is to have any significance beyond personal indulgence. A necessary and sufficient prerequisite for both parties is a "willing suspension of disbelief," since dialogue cannot wait until trust is established, but is in itself a means of creating trust.

Dialogue requires honesty, candor, and courage if it is to accomplish any of its objectives, but mainly it needs the courage to convey and receive the truth (or truths). For the Palestinians, it takes tremendous courage to transcend the pain of the moment and to overcome the constraints of their oppression, whose brutality is capable of generating responses of hatred and revenge. In overcoming the temptation to succumb to the sense of historical injustice done to them, the Palestinians are capable of making the "imaginative leap" into a vision of future peace. The Israelis are also required to exercise the courage required to swim against the tide of official policy and public opinion—often to the extent of defying the law—in order to participate in actualizing this vision of peace. Both must have the will and commitment to maintain dialogue and bring it to a positive conclusion.

In spite of all the preceding, dialogue has its own not insignificant pitfalls and dangers, which are capable of generating misunderstanding and conflict if not fully understood and consciously avoided. The following is a summary of some of the major hazards:

1. The will to appeal to or please the other by avoiding or misrepresenting real concerns, which may be potentially disputatious or disconcerting. Such attempts are essentially hypocritical and dishonest and are easily exposed as false complaisance, which can blur the issues and contribute to mistrust. Most accusations of deception and "hidden agendas" stem from such lack of candor.

2. Failure to recognize asymmetry and differences. In con-

temporary Palestinian-Israeli realities, a glaring situation of imbalance has to be admitted as an essential factor in the dialogue—namely, in the discrepancy between occupier and occupied. In addition, Palestinians engaged in dialogue have the assurance of a clear political program with the support of an overwhelming majority and a national consensus. Israelis, so far, remain a minority seeking political validation within their own establishment and society. This double disequilibrium must be accounted for in the attribution of value and weight to statements and positions, as well as in perpetrating a false sense of normalization, which contradicts the blatantly "abnormal" condition of occupation.

3. Manipulation of dialogue for specific ends. Often narrow party interests or personal ambitions impose themselves on the broader concerns of the participants and are allowed to influence (and distort) the natural course of dialogue.

4. Misplaced priorities and forced agreement. Neither side must impose its priorities on the other or adopt the other's priorities, whether consciously or inadvertently. Separateness and differences have to be appreciated and admitted, especially in political agendas, before joint concerns and areas of concurrence are explored and expanded.

5. Unconscious assimilation. In addition to priorities and agendas, discourse and tone must maintain their separate authenticity as the genuine expression of each part without undergoing a process of absorption, which may lead to delegitimization within and alienation from respective constituencies.

6. Hypothetical projection. In their zeal to prepare for future developments and contingencies, dialogue participants anticipate or project hypothetical obstacles and future scenarios at the cost of current and pressing problems. The urgency of the present cannot be ignored or postponed pending the theoretical solution of potential problems in the future. Anticipation is constructive only when rooted in a firm understanding of its present sources and time frame.

7. Derailment into side issues and digressions. Detours and evasions are liable to dissipate energies and distract attention from focal points. Clear and logically coherent dialogue strate-

gies, as the central motivation and driving force of dialogue, must be agreed upon and maintained.

8. Dialogue as a means of obtaining concessions. The use of dialogue opportunities to obtain prenegotiation concessions may invalidate dialogue itself and create suspicion and reticence, while undermining the peace process.

9. Dialogue as catharsis. If dialogue is used to assuage or diffuse the sense of guilt that some Israelis feel at the oppression of the occupation or at their inability to bring about effective change, then it becomes an escape rather than a corrective force. Political self-indulgence then replaces concrete strategy and commitment to peace as the operative term for dialogue.

10. Exhibitionistic one-up-manship. Historical distortions and recrimination can set dialogue on a dead-end course. Similarly, pain and suffering can neither be compared nor quantified, for the uniqueness of each experience places it beyond the scope of political discourse.

11. Threat to legitimacy. Dialogue cannot succeed if each side attempts to undermine the legitimacy or power base of the other.

12. Dialogue vs. negotiations. Participants in dialogue must not attempt to usurp the role of legitimate representatives and interlocutors. Nor can dialogue replace the real process of negotiations, but it must lay a solid foundation for negotiations and a positive momentum toward peaceful resolution.

The pitfalls of dialogue are further aggravated when dialogue usurps the role of negotiations or becomes a structured stage in the peace process. In the metamorphosis of Palestinian-Israeli dialogue and as an extension and direct expression of its political context, the term "dialogue" has acquired a specific semantic significance. The five points of U. S. Secretary of State James Baker employ the term to denote, with almost clinical precision, a meeting between an Israeli and a Palestinian delegation, in Cairo, some time after a tripartite meeting among the Israeli and Egyptian and American foreign ministers, and some time before elections in the occupied territories are held. Here, "dialogue" itself becomes an issue having lost its voluntary dimension as a willful pursuit of human understanding through direct communication. Instead, it has become immersed in political contention, emerging as a microcosmic encapsulation of the essence of the Palestinian-Israeli conflict.

To the Israeli government, this dialogue is another means for the exercise of domination, for devising a form of "legitimacy" in perpetuating the occupation, for isolating the issue by turning it into an "internal" Israeli problem for the denial of PLO legitimacy, and for the negation of the Palestinians' right to self-determination and statehood. To the Palestinians and the PLO, this dialogue is a means of launching a genuine peace process as a preparatory step toward the international peace conference, for ending the occupation, for demonstrating the unity of the Palestinian people under occupation and in exile, for asserting PLO legitimacy as the sole legitimate representative and interlocutor for the Palestinian people, for affirming the Palestinian right to self-determination leading to independent statehood. The provisos, conditions, and interpretations imposed on this "dialogue" by the Israeli government are a means of maintaining the status quo (of the occupation) through digressions and evasive tactics, seeking to avoid the challenge of peace and to buy time for the brutal suppression of the *intifada*. By accepting the principle of elections and dialogue, the PLO (specifically the PNC and Central Council) is pursuing a path of realism, flexibility, and historical responsibility in pursuit of an equitable, peaceful resolution on the basis of symmetry, reciprocity, and international legitimacy.

In particular, Israel's attempts at excluding PLO participation in dialogue and the PLO's clear selection and announcement of Palestinian participants are a repetition of the mistake that has contributed historically to the aggravation of the conflict—the circumvention of the Palestinian will and legitimacy. Its attempts at restricting the agenda to the "elections" issue are further repetitions of the mistake of trying to sidestep central issues. Its attempts at excluding the participation of Palestinians from East Jerusalem are a means of legitimizing the annexation of the territories occupied by force and through war. Its attempts at preventing international participation are a recurrence of the mistake of excessive isolationism, diminution, and subversion of international legitimacy and guarantees. Its attempts at reducing the whole "dialogue" to the lowest common denominator of

Israeli priorities and domination are an exercise in futility and misdirection. Thus by extracting from dialogue all the principles and meaningful substance that are capable of rendering it effective, Israel is destroying the most basic tenets of conflict resolution through dialogue. By excluding the only partner capable of taking decisions and implementing them, Israel is distorting the essence of dialogue by eliminating the second-person pronoun from its discourse and restricting it to the convolution of the first-person obsessive. Throughout the protean history of dialogue in the Palestinian-Israeli experience, Israel has finally managed the unprecedented and semantically impossible travesty of the ultimate transmutation of dialogue into monologue.

The current impasse in the peace process is due primarily to this distortion of the principles of dialogue and to the excessive Israeli control and restrictions on its scope and dimensions. The challenge of the 1990s with its global readjustments and peaceful resolutions of long-standing conflicts demands a stance of courage, imagination, and historical responsibility. It is hoped that Israel will rise to the challenge of true dialogue.

8

Confronting Evil:
A Prerequisite for Dialogue

HAIM GORDON

Today, in the midst of the forceful and often brutal Israeli oppression of the Palestinian uprising, I believe that genuine dialogue between Jews and Palestinians can be established only on the basis of a willingness to confront evil and to struggle against it. I also believe that is the reason why dialogue is so scarce, because few Jews in Israel are willing to confront the evil that we are directly responsible for. There are small movements that do confront evil, like Yesh Gvul or Women in Black. But the public response to these movements reveals how most Jews flee such a confrontation.

Consider Women in Black. Initiated by seven women in Jerusalem in the early spring of 1988 as an ongoing demonstration against Israel's unjust occupation of the West Bank and the Gaza Strip, Women in Black numbered in early 1990 more than one thousand Jewish women (and a few Arab women) who demonstrate in every major city in Israel and in other locations — altogether at more than thirty locations — every Friday from 1 to 2 P.M. The women are clothed totally in black and stand at busy intersections all over Israel holding signs saying: Stop the Occupation.

The basic message of Women in Black is that the Israeli occupation of the West Bank and Gaza is immoral; it is wrong to deny the Palestinians living there their freedom; it is wrong to exploit and oppress them; and since evil deeds, in addition to inflicting undue suffering, corrupt the performer of such deeds, we Israelis must stop the occupation immediately. Otherwise we will slowly demolish our democratic regime and the values upon which the Jewish state was established. All verbal quibbling is irrelevant; Israel must pull out now.

The important point about Women in Black is that they are a weekly reminder of the evil we are doing. Unfortunately, they have had almost no success in encouraging most Israelis to confront evil. The opposite is frequently the case. Very often right-wing extremists curse these women, using ethnically explicit curses and often calling them whores of the PLO. At times demonstrating women have been beaten and shoved, and their signs have been torn from their hands and destroyed. Probably because many members of the Israeli police force do not agree with the goals of their demonstration, Women in Black get limited and sporadic police protection. And most Israelis, including many persons affiliated with the Israeli media, pass by these demonstrating women without relating to their message. In short, many Jews bask in indifference.

The fact that most Israelis and all members of the Israeli government placidly accept the evil deeds that Israeli military forces are doing in the occupied territories blocks almost all possibilities of dialogue. This blocking of dialogue is most evident in five main areas. First, there is almost no dialogue between Jews who accept the daily oppression that includes the killing, wounding, and beating of Palestinians and these oppressed Palestinians. Second, there is almost no dialogue among Jews about the Palestinian uprising, about the evil deeds that we are daily instigating. Third, there is no interfaith dialogue between religious Jews and Muslims. Fourth, there is almost no official dialogue between representatives of Israel and representatives of the Palestinians, in this case Yasir Arafat and the PLO. And finally, Israel's adamant policy seems to have closed all avenues of dialogue about peace in the Middle East between the representatives of Israel and officials in the governments of its close Western allies. Before examining how this patent lack of dialogue helps perpetuate evil deeds, let us look a bit closer at these five areas.

Dialogue is a meeting between persons who live their freedom. Rarely can it occur in a situation of oppression—there are even fewer chances for dialogue between Jews and Arabs when Arab freedom is violently and brutally oppressed by Jews, such as occurs daily in the occupied territories since the beginning of the Palestinian uprising, the *intifada*. What is more, if dialogue does occur in a situation of oppression it will soon erode that situation. Many persons sense this intuitively. Consequently, Jews who support the daily oppression of Palestinians will fear to meet Palestinians in dialogue. They sense that a dialogical encounter will diminish the force of their dominating and domineering political position. Few Jews sense that one result of this callous position is that by denying the Palestinians their freedom, these Jews are limiting their own possibility to relate dialogically and to live in freedom. (This is, of course, merely another perspective of the master-slave dialectic, mentioned by Hegel.)

Since the beginning of the *intifada*, there is also very little dialogue among Jews about the situation in the occupied territories. Two antidialogical responses have emerged. The first are strong verbal attacks by right-wing politicians and their fanatic followers upon those few Jews who initiate dialogue with Palestinians or who, like Women in Black, reject the evil we are doing. Jews who work for dialogue are called traitors, Jew-haters, PLO lovers, in addition to being cursed and at times physically attacked. Quite often right-wing politicians and their diabolical faithful have even stated that these prodialogue Jews deserve death. Such violence-oriented demagoguery, such blatant evil, eradicates almost all possibilities of inter-Jewish dialogue.

The second response, which leads many Jews to ignore the possibility of internal Jewish dialogue upon key issues, is the attempt to always be attuned to what is currently called "the consensus"—Martin Heidegger would have called it the voice of the "they." The "they" is the voice of idle talk that engulfs most persons' everyday being and does not allow a person to relate authentically to one's existential situation. The voice of the "they" will always interfere with a person's attempt to assume a personal courageous moral stance. Thus, when one is always attuned to following "the consensus," one forfeits the possibility of relating authentically to other persons or to the situation in which one finds oneself. Evil is accepted as an act of fate; genuine dialogue becomes an impossibility.

The lack of interfaith dialogue in Israel is appalling—especially if one recalls that in this land members of all three monotheistic faiths worship what each one calls the One God in places that each faith designates as holy. Thus Jews, Christians, and Muslims live as next-door neighbors in a land they call holy—in Jerusalem, Jews and Christians daily hear the muezzin calling Muslims to prayer, Christians and Muslims hear Jews praying and dancing at the Wailing Wall, Jews and Muslims hear Christian church bells ringing—but being neighbors does not lead most adherents to engage in any meaningful interfaith dialogue. There are many reasons for this sad situation, probably the most significant being that all three faiths have no few dogmatic, myopic, and at times fanatic leaders.

But one should immediately add that the role of Israel's religious leaders in perpetuating the lack of interfaith dialogue is predominant, because Israel is the current political ruler of the land. Unfortunately, the religious leaders in Israel—for instance, both the chief Ashkenazi and the chief Sephardic rabbis—accept and support the political oppression of Palestinians. They accept Israel's disregard for Palestinian civil rights. Other rabbis are at the forefront of the evil being done to Arabs; Meir Kahane was an example. Furthermore, these rabbinical racists and bigots, who have encouraged and supported many evil acts, have never been criticized by the Israeli religious establishment. Now, with the outbreak of the *intifada* and its daily toll of violence and casualties, the most outspoken religious leaders have adopted an extremist stance and interfaith dialogue has become a naive dream.

The ongoing irresponsibility of the Israeli religious establishment in the area of interfaith dialogue should not discourage lay people; some lay people understand this. There have been some serious attempts by Jewish religious groups to encourage interfaith dialogue. Unfortunately, these attempts have had little impact upon the antidialogical atmosphere that currently prevails. What is more, even prodialogue religious Jews have rarely spoken out forcefully against the evil deeds done by Jews against Arabs, or in other words they have not given their whole being to the dialogical process.

Israel's refusal to meet with the accepted representatives of the Palestinian people, the PLO, is becoming a ludicrous stupidity. Already, Israel is negotiating with the PLO through representatives of Egypt and the United States, so why not speak directly? The truth is that many Israelis have spoken directly and some have been convicted for it, while others have gone completely free. The only reason I can see why the Israeli government refuses to talk with the PLO is that by engaging in such a dialogue it would have to admit that it is talking with the representatives of a nation, and that would mean giving up land for that nation to exist. In short, evil intentions—in this case greed and the wish to continue to oppress Palestinians—blocks this much needed dialogue. One outcome of this stupidity is that Israeli leaders can no longer meaningfully discuss the international situation in the Middle East with Western leaders. There is a limit to the amount of evil intentions dressed up as a wish for security that even these leaders can swallow.

I have been working for Jewish-Arab dialogue in the Middle East for more than a decade, and I have documented quite a bit of my work.[1] At first, in 1979, I attempted to teach Jews and Arabs to realize the dialogical philosophy of Martin Buber in their everyday life. The first two years of this six-year attempt were a rather euphoric period; many Jews and Arabs in Israel were excited about the signing of the Israeli-Egyptian peace treaty and about the possibility of visiting Egypt, which until then was the land of an Arab enemy. With the fading of that excitement, and especially after the brutal Israeli invasion of Lebanon, it became much more difficult to engage in dialogue. Later, as the oppression of Palestinians in the occupied territories became more cruel, there was less and less support in the Israeli establishment, and I suspect in the Israeli public, for any efforts of dialogue.

One of the basic elements of Buberian dialogue is that in such an encounter persons do not try to manipulate each other or the conversation. Rather there is an openness, a willingness to listen, to learn, to confront the other and to confront issues, and most important, to give of oneself wholly to the other. In genuine dialogue one is not striving to make an impression, but rather one is always attempting to speak straightforwardly, to give one's entire being. Empathy, Buber stressed, is not dialogue, for empathy is not a confronting of the other, it is not a giving of oneself wholly to the other. In dialogue one does not identify with the other, one relates fully to the other.

During the six years that I worked on various funded projects whose goal was encouraging Jewish-Arab dialogue, I became aware of the spiritual enhancement that accompanies the realizing of Buber's dialogical thought. As Buber indicated, a new dimension of personal and spiritual existence can open up to a person who can relate to God, to the world, and to the persons whom one meets as a "Thou." But I also learned the severe limitations of Buber's dialogical philosophy. Put briefly, Buber gives very little guidance as to how one can forcefully confront the various manifestations of evil that one encounters. With all my experience in realizing Buber's thought, with all my learning from his significant writings, I do not see how one can reach genuine dialogue with a racist or a fervent fanatic. Furthermore, Buber gives very little guidance as to how one can and should act in the political realm, and he almost totally ignores the influence of economic exigencies on political developments.[2]

Thus Buber never suggested that together with one's willingness to engage in dialogue, one must be willing to take a forceful stance against the evil that prevails. Perhaps the saddest example of such an approach in Buber's personal history is that although he criticized the Nazis, he never forcefully condemned the Nazis and their unbelievable atrocities. Make no mistake, Martin Buber was a courageous person; yet he sought ways of evading what the situation at times demanded—that he, the acclaimed philosopher of dialogue, forcefully condemn the ugly manifestations of evil.

In this respect Buber's deeds and a few of his later writings were not faithful to some of the basic insights that appear in his most important work, *I and Thou*. If dialogue, as explained at length in *I and Thou*, is a relating of a person as a whole being to the other, one cannot be whole if one ignores evil or evades confronting it, especially when its manifestations are evident daily. Thus, in Buber's ontology the relationship between dialogue and the confronting of evil is dialectic. I am arguing that the wish to relate dialogically can lead to a confronting of evil, and not only that one needs to confront evil in order to relate dialogically.

But whichever way one approaches the dialectic of dialogue and evil, in the context of Israeli-Palestinian dialogue the present situation demands that I, as a Jew, must be willing to tell a Jewish racist who hates all Arabs and wants to oppress them or to forcefully exile them from their land—and there are no few such Jewish racists, they even have some representatives in the Knesset—clearly and emphatically: you are evil, and I will daily struggle against you!

Here is where some of my criticisms of the Palestinians who are working for Israeli-Palestinian dialogue emerge. As representatives of a people who are struggling for political freedom, those Palestinians who wish to end Israeli oppression and exploitation by peaceful means are to be admired. They are working under an immense strain, since often they cannot stem the rage of their people who daily suffer from unjust Israeli deeds, or from beatings and killings by Israeli soldiers. But this very difficult situation demands a clarity of expression that is frequently lacking in the public responses of some Palestinian leaders who work for Israeli-Palestinian dialogue. When asked about manifestations of evil among Palestinians, some of these dialogue-oriented persons are apologetic. They seem to have overlooked the fact that apologetics is not a manner of confronting evil; furthermore, apologetics will rarely encourage dialogue.

In other words, the struggle for dialogue is extremely difficult, because it must include the struggle against fanatical zealots and persons who encourage and spread intolerance and hatred in one's own nation. Apologizing for these ardent disseminators of hatred and prejudice is not a confronting of evil, and will not encourage the trust of one's partner in dialogue.

Let me give an example of such an encouraging of hatred of Arabs by Jews. What follows are excerpts from an article that appeared in the newspaper *Hatzofeh* on September 8, 1989. *Hatzofeh* is affiliated with one of the Jewish religious political parties. The article is by Yitzchak Strolovitz:

> The sons of Ishmael have been fighting against us for one hundred years. Even though they have twenty-three independent states, they are spending millions of dollars to attack the Jewish state. They want to kill and destroy the inhabitants of [the Jewish] state and have drawn their inspiration from the Palestinian covenant, which has in turn drawn its inspiration from [Hitler's] *Mein Kampf*. The wish to murder and hatred are in their blood from childhood.

Needless to say, the reader of such an article will understand that one must hate these bloodthirsty Arabs. I should perhaps add that such writing is quite common in *Hatzofeh*, and that this blatant racism by Jewish religious leaders has seldom been attacked publicly by other Israeli journalists or by Jewish politicians. Unfortunately, it seems to be acceptable in both Arab and Jewish societies that religious fanatics can write racist statements at will, without encountering the public censure of so-called liberal politicians, with hardly ever being attacked as racists or fanatics by their compatriots. Such an acceptance is just another manner of legitimizing racism. Furthermore, in Jewish society it is very often these Jewish fanatics and racists who contribute substantially to the antidialogical mood that currently prevails in Israel. Thus by not forcefully confronting and rejecting evil statements, such as cited above, statements that are often spread by the Israeli religious establishment, Israeli politicians and citizens are daily supporting those who wish to legitimize Jewish racism.

In summary, two points need to be emphasized. First, the overwhelming majority of Jewish writers, university professors, journalists, artists, and other intellectuals in Israel are daily shirking the task that history demands of this elite: sensitivity to injustice and the condemnation of evil. To judge by their response to our oppression of the Palestinian struggle for freedom, one can only conclude that most members of this elite in Israel are myopic and cowardly, insensitive and callous. For instance, in Beer Sheva, where I reside, there are forty to fifty women on the faculty of Ben Gurion University. Only one of them has joined the weekly demonstration of Women in Black in Beer Sheva. Nor has any member of the eight-hundred-member faculty of Ben Gurion University, except the author of this article, spoken out forcefully and bluntly in public against the evil we are daily doing to the Palestinians.

And finally, this cowardice on the part of the Jewish intellectual elite is symptomatic of the degraded moral situation in Israel. By banishing from our daily life and from our political approach the possibility of dialogue and of struggling against evil, we Jews are ruining our own spiritual existence. We are destroying our ability to live in the light of the sayings of the Hebrew prophets. We are discarding our heritage, selling our birthright for a pot of lentil soup.

One can only hope and pray that those voices speaking out for dialogue in Israel will soon be heeded.

NOTES

1. My first three years of working for Jewish-Arab dialogue are described and discussed in Haim Gordon, *Dance, Dialogue, and Despair: Existentialist Philosophy and Education for Peace in Israel* (University of Alabama Press, 1986). A discussion of some of my additional work can be found in my articles in Haim Gordon and Leonard Grob, *Education for Peace: Testimonies from World Religions* (Maryknoll, N.Y.: Orbis Books, 1987).

2. I have discussed this problem of Buber's philosophy in Haim Gordon, *Make Room for Dreams: Spiritual Challenges to Zionism* (Westport, Conn.: Greenwood Press, 1989).

SECTION 5

PALESTINIAN WOMEN AND DIALOGUE

One of the best hidden secret forces behind the success of the *intifada*, the Palestinian uprising, is the determination of Palestinian women. Before the *intifada*, slowly, by much hard grassroot work, Palestinian women on the West Bank and in the Gaza Strip set up organizations to protect their rights and to help them find their place, economically and socially, in the macho-oriented Palestinian society. Naturally, when the *intifada* became a reality, these organizations could continue the educational mission they had undertaken while also educating for freedom from Israeli oppression. The result has been that the *intifada* is an uprising that includes women, together with the men and boys. It is truly a populist uprising.

The above paragraph makes it sound too easy. For a Palestinian woman to assert her freedom in Palestinian society is an arduous lifelong task. Deeply ingrained mores and many religious injunctions favor male domination and relegate women to a secondary or minor role. In addition, women, like all Palestinians, are oppressed by the Israeli military establishment. It is therefore no surprise that many women who struggled for emancipation have undergone much personal suffering during their long march to freedom. Perhaps that is one of the reasons why these women value dialogue at all levels of human interaction. They know; they have learned that only through nonmanipulative conversation do they have a chance of asserting their freedom in the chauvinistic world that encompasses them.

Make no mistake. As Zahira Kamal wryly notes in her essay, Israeli society is also macho-oriented. This male chauvinism prevails not only among the male Orthodox Jews who daily pray to God and thank God for not creating them a woman. It is also very prominent among secular Jews. The worshiping of the military golem in Israel is just one aspect of this deep-rooted machoism. Hence, Mariam Mar'i and Zahira Kamal are not only struggling against the antifeminism of their own Palestinian society, they have also had to cope with the degrading male chauvinism emanating from the dominant Jewish Israeli society.

Mariam Mar'i is one of only three Palestinian women who are Israeli citizens who hold a Ph.D. She teaches part-time in the School of Education at Haifa University, and spends most of her time educating Arab women at the Early Childhood Educational Center for the Arab Child in Acre. She established this center and is currently its general director. Zahira Kamal is a leading Palestinian feminist. She is chairwoman of the Palestinian Federation of Women's Action Committees, and in this capacity has been frequently jailed and interrogated by the Israel Security Service. She has often been under house arrest or been told that she is not allowed to leave the confines of the city of Jerusalem, where she resides.

In addition to their broad range of activities, both women have been very active in Israeli-Palestinian dialogue. They are clearsighted, however, in their evaluation of the results of their working for dialogue. They state forcefully that without recognition of the rights of Palestinians as human beings, dialogue is quite often an exercise in futility. Hence they stress the importance of immediately discontinuing the oppression of Palestinians, be it Palestinians residing in Israel who are Israeli citizens or Palestinians in the West Bank and Gaza Strip. One senses that since they have partially overcome male oppression in their own society, they are willing to struggle against all forms of oppression. It seems as if their personal history, which they partially disclose in their essays, is a source of personal valorization and empowerment.

9

A Palestinian View of the Quest for Palestinian-Israeli Dialogue: Accounting for Aspirations and Fears

Zahira Kamal

In the arena of human conflict, words somehow acquire a measurable degree of significance. Terms like "dialogue" and "negotiations" need not be defined to initiate exchanges of views and positions when conducted between amicable parties. For conflicting parties, however, precise definitions of these and similar terms become important. But however these definitions are formulated, the initiation and success of exchanges rest on the real intentions and designs, concealed or publicized, of the conflicting parties.

My consent to participate in this book on Palestinian-Israeli dialogue was made in good faith. It is the faith that rests on the conviction that there are some Palestinians and some Israelis who genuinely wish to conduct a process of purposeful dialogue, however defined. But since there are others who currently do not hold the same desires, I feel it necessary to address myself to all concerned with the conflict. For this purpose and for the purpose of clarity, I shall proceed by presenting my own definitions.

To me and to many of my Palestinian colleagues, dialogue is a form of purposeful and constructive contact wherein a free exchange of viewpoints takes place. But then there are other forms of contact between conflicting parties. There is the contact between the occupier and the occupied, and also the contact between the two sides of a negotiating table. Differences among subjugation, dialogue, and negotiation are discernible, at least to my mind.

Whereas dialogue and negotiation are processes that are voluntary and freely undertaken, subjugation as occupation is very much a coercive process. Furthermore, the negotiating process inherently implies an a priori commitment (at least to oneself) to reach a favorable conclusion within the compromising framework of "give and take." Dialogue, on the other hand, carries no such commitment, but only the uncertain promise of freely conceded changes in the conceptions of either or both parties. Another discernible difference between negotiation and dialogue is that the former is a process conducted among freely chosen representatives of each of the two conflicting parties. Dialogue, on the other hand, can be conducted between any one or more grouping within each conflicting party with any one or more grouping of the other party.

Subjugation as occupation and its maintenance is the conscious decision of one party of a conflict. The initiation of dialogue and its continuation, however, result from the conscious and free choice of both parties. By definition, then, dialogue cannot take place unless it is desired by both parties.

An outsider to the conflict might be excused for detecting, in the above, elements of obsession with detail and precision. But then the outsider cannot be blamed for being confronted by an ever-evolving tragedy, often irrationally acted out by protagonists with deeply engraved sensitivities. It is unfair to expect all outsiders to be familiar with all the intricate webs that time has woven around this conflict. After all, the protagonists themselves have not infrequently fallen victims to the numerous vicious circles they helped to create. If the Israelis managed to re-create their Israel after two thousand years, why should not the Palestinians re-create their Palestine only a few decades after its disappearance? If the Israeli objective is to draw in a dozen million of world Jewry to this land, why should not the few million Palestinians thrown out be allowed to return? If Israel cannot survive but by the force of arms, why then did Sparta fall? If your writ is holy, who has the human wisdom to judge that it is holier than mine? If your suffering and persecution was immense, as indeed it was, then by what heavenly or human writ was my suffering and persecution ordained?

But then not all outsiders to the conflict are guilt-free innocent bystanders. The creation of the state of Israel was largely brought about as a consequence of the persecution of European Jews by much of Christian Europe of the distant and near past. To the Palestinians, the European resolution of the problem of Jewish persecution is astonishingly peculiar and unjust. For the most elementary form of human justice dictates that when a vicious crime is committed (as in the case of the persecution of European Jews), justice for the victim ought to be sought at the scene of the crime (i.e., Europe) and not elsewhere (such as remote Palestine). Furthermore, it is the criminals (among Europeans) who ought to pay for their crimes, not someone else — least of all the Palestinians who are innocent of European crimes. Above all, justice ought to annul the effects of the crime (in this case, Jewish insecurity in Europe) and not aid in the removal of the victim (the Jews) away from the scene of the crime.

This is precisely why Palestinians find some European attitudes toward Israeli security as being nothing short of hypocrisy. For were these concerns genuine enough, European efforts would have been directed at making Europe more secure for the European Jews. Were this the case, many Jews would not have fled Europe to seek security elsewhere. The Palestinians profoundly feel that they have been left to carry the heavy burden of European guilt toward the Jews. The innocent Palestinian is made to pay for European crimes. As if that was not sufficient, many segments of the European mass media went on to paint a horrendous picture of the Palestinians, equating with terrorism their struggle for their rights. Coming from the inventors of concentration camps and gas chambers, some aspects of European morality as occasionally portrayed in their mass media amaze and indeed shock the Palestinian mind.

The tragedy of the Palestinians in the recent past appears ready to repeat itself in the not too distant future. Again, the alleged crime, criminal, and victim are European—namely, the issue of insecurity of Russian Jews in the Soviet Union. Again, calls are out today for the resolution of this insecurity by the transfer of these Jews to what remains of the land of former Palestine—the West Bank and the Gaza Strip. It is remarkable and a sad reflection on humanity that these calls should come out strongest from none other than Jews, themselves the very victims of past European persecutions. For it is some elements among the Israelis who nowadays call for the transfer of Palestinians to neighboring Jordan to make room for the Jews fleeing insecurity and lack of opportunity within Russia itself. Yet Palestinians are again called upon to bear more crosses of guilt and pay for someone else's crimes. Such insensitivity toward the Palestinians (and indeed the Jordanians) emanating from people who are supposedly very sensitive in other respects (e.g., to Jewish security) is simply astounding.

The arguments are indeed endless; the painful logic is devastatingly powerful. Yet the sensitivities, fears, and suffering are real, profound, and persistent. The reality of the Palestinian-Israeli conflict is that there is hardly any Israeli aspiration or fear that does not find a corresponding Palestinian aspiration and fear. After all, these human elements cannot be the sole prerogative of any single race, nation, or religious creed. It is my deep conviction that Israel and the Israelis will never achieve their longed for security as long as the Palestinians have none. This is neither a threat nor a promise, but the mere comment of insecure, dispossessed Palestinians so tragically made to pay by both the victims and perpetrators of some other monumental crime; a comment by Palestinians who, like their Israeli counterparts, refuse to abandon their right to a secure homeland, the very land of their fathers.

The logic of our conflict does not differ from that of any other human conflict. Its ultimate resolution can come either through the total submission of either party or through compromise. Total submission cannot be confined to its military interpretation; it also encompasses the abandonment of all hope and aspirations. The clearest example comes from the two thousand years of Jewish diaspora; it was the hope and aspirations of Jews to return that eventually brought about the re-creation of their Israel. In this respect the Palestinians are nowhere near submission despite their current almost hopeless military situation.

It is precisely because of all the above that I am a firm believer in Palestinian-Israeli dialogue. My past and present experiences, modest as they are, have aided my resolve to pursue this goal not only as an end in itself but also as a means to resolving our tragic conflict. Currently, the positive manner of resolution can to my mind find only one form: a secure Palestinian homeland on parts of former Palestine adjacent to a secure Israel. With this goal in mind I believe that most Palestinians are now both desirous and ready to initiate and develop dialogue with the Israelis. It is heartening that despite being still a minority, an increasing number of Israelis have the same enthusiasm for dialogue with Palestinians. But it is my observation that the bulk of Israeli opinion is still far less concerned with dialogue and is more preoccupied with other aspects of the conflict. One such aspect involves the absence of recognition of the reality of the Palestinians as a national entity, which includes their aspirations and inalienable rights to choose their own leaders and spokesmen. Another relates to what "concessions" if any the Israelis should "grant" in the as yet nonexistent negotiations. A third Israeli issue finds its supporters totally engrossed in their dreams of expanding the current land of Israel by the total expulsion of the remaining Palestinians.

I would be less than candid if I or many of my Palestinian colleagues were to claim that our commitment to dialogue was always as firm or as deep. In my case my belief in dialogue developed from almost nonexistence to its present form as a result of more than a decade of social and cultural field work among Palestinian women, close but certainly nonintimate contacts with occupation authorities, countless discussions with my colleagues, and an increasing contact with more and more Israeli individuals and groups of varied political beliefs.

My contact with the Israeli occupation authorities dates back to August 1979, when I was first locked up in administrative detention. This was followed by several preventive detentions a few years later. For most of the 1980s I was confined by military orders within the limits of Jerusalem except for special permission to attend my teaching work at a United Nations teacher training college in nearby Ramallah. I am currently served with an order banning me from travel abroad for a period of three months. My case was officially adopted by Amnesty International as a case of a "prisoner of conscience."

I confess that as a Palestinian, my treatment by the occupation authorities made me among the fortunate few. I was never physically molested in prison or had my bones softened for resisting violent arrest. I was never fatally injured while descending prison steps or shot at by a remote yet dangerously threatening security sniper. Above all I was not dragged out at night and deported outside my Palestine.

In comparison, I was even more fortunate than my interrogators themselves. Because my activities were always open, they could not get out of me any new information or major insight. But to me, the interrogation sessions were very illuminating despite their boring repetitiveness. It surprised me how much my interrogators were obsessed by their persistent aim of breaking my faith in anything that was of value, be it social, political, or ethical. Theirs was an all-out crusade to brainwash me into accepting that all I did and all I believed in was in vain. But as is the case with thousands of Palestinians and many thousands of other struggling human souls throughout the world, my case was typical. Imprisonment and interrogation, physical and mental suffering, will often fortify one's faith in what one perceives as justice and freedom from persecution. I have not been the first to go through the agony, nor will I be the last to adhere to a just cause.

It is worthwhile pointing out one more trait that characterized my interrogators. It is their approach of stereotyping the Palestinian character to conform conveniently with previously held notions and concepts. To them, the Palestinian is an Arab and as such is a dirty coward, treacherous and incapable of any initiative. Worse still, the Palestinian female is a weakling Arab who is fully subservient to the Arab male. As such the ignorance of my interrogators privileged me with a double insult. It was to their surprise that I fitted neither of their images. As an Arab woman seeking equality with males within Palestinian society, my struggle has been long and arduous, but nevertheless rewarding. In this respect it amused me to discover that I was better informed about Palestinian women than were my interrogators.

In all fairness, had my contacts with Israelis been confined to their military occupation forces, my view of the conflict would have remained a one-sided affair regardless of the oppressive weight of the occupation. It has been my good fortune and indeed my privilege that I was among the very few Palestinians under occupation to have had an early contact with a different facet of Israeli society. Initially and until the mid-1980s this contact was confined to academics and to the liberal Israeli intelligentsia. It later widened to include human rights activists, who to my surprise at the time were keen on securing justice for Palestinian cases with equal vigor as that pursued for other cases elsewhere. Later the dialogue was widened to include the circle of activists in the women's rights movement. It was particularly satisfying for me to compare with other Israeli women a wide range of similarities in viewpoints. Currently, Palestinian-Israeli dialogue is finding its way into labor movements and even among kibbutz societies.

Not surprisingly, the dominating themes ensuing out of our sessions of dialogue were common to both sides. It suffices to mention a few. The first that comes to mind is fear—such as the fear of an Israeli mother for her son taken into the army; the fear of imprisonment and torture felt by a Palestinian mother for her son. Another common feature was the unrealistic image held by each party of the other, an image that was physically confined by the lens of the television photographer and the pen of the script editor of the various media. Yet another achievement of dialogue was better appreciation by both sides of the differences between terrorism and freedom fighting. It was not difficult in many cases to define hijackings and the murder of innocent civilians as terrorism. Nor was it difficult for some Israelis to accept that Palestinians had the right to use military force if need be to achieve their rights. Yet a common complaint emphasized with equal bitterness by both sides was the loneliness and almost dispiriting feeling of being in a minority within one's own society. As a Palestinian, this lonely feeling of being a supporter of Palestinian-Israeli dialogue has eased tremendously ever since the early days of the *intifada*. Our cause within our own society has since been significantly relieved of this burden by the official PLO recognition of Israel's right to exist. Much of the Palestinian opposition to dialogue that stemmed from the fear that it may lead to submission or a process of negotiations between unequal parties has now subsided.

Many Israelis suspiciously point out that the average Palestinian they hear today calling for dialogue, negotiations, and peaceful coexistence is the very same Palestinian who until a couple of decades ago was cheering to the slogan of throwing the Israelis into the sea. These Israelis genuinely ask whether this is a real change or a mere tactic. My answer is that the change is authentic, substantial, and strategic in its form and implications. Those who doubt my word can find out for themselves by simply talking to the Palestinians.

The above change in the Palestinian political outlook is not the sudden and theatrical metamorphosis that some Israelis claim it to be. It is simply a reflection of a development process of the politicized Palestinian toward the real and possible, away from the self-defeating and consuming turmoil of vengeance and self-pity. It is no longer the Palestinian who like the wronged King Lear howls vengeance hitherto untold yet unreal. It is no longer the Palestinian who is swayed by the eloquence of hollow oratories and fruitless pledges made by others. It is no longer the Palestinian who seeks suicidal missions that end up in self-destruction.

Assertive Palestinians of today have not acquired confidence from the illusive laurels of long-sought-after military victories. Their confidence emanates more from deep faith in their cause: the same patient faith that propels a fearless unarmed *intifada* against the might of the Israeli military machine.

It is a sad comment that the flight of the Palestinians away from illusions and self-pity is yet to be matched by a corresponding change in Israeli attitudes. The stark reality is that the bulk of Israelis seem at best to ignore the Palestinian national identity, while many others still seek its annihilation. The bulk of

Israeli opinion is as yet not one of accommodation with the Palestinians.

The survival of the Israeli state and Palestinian national identity have for far too long been viewed by the majority of Israelis as a zero-sum affair. The more that Palestinians clung to their identity, the more their political association came to the fore; Palestinian aspirations to a homeland equal the downfall of Israel; Palestinian aspirations and political rights equal loss of Israeli security; Palestinian struggle, even when peaceful, equals terrorism; and so forth. Like the ghosts that bedeviled Macbeth, Palestinian identity has haunted much of the politics of Israeli leadership ever since 1948. No utterances, actions, or wars would seem to wish them away.

To us Palestinians, the resolution of this Israeli view does not lie in ingenious methods of equation solving. It simply resides in the rejection of the entire Israeli equation as a fallacy of equating inequalities. While both Palestinian aspirations and Israeli security are legitimate parameters, equating them in a zero-sum fashion is wrong and misleading. Furthermore, one cannot formulate the conflict in a paradoxical manner, maintain it all along, then proceed to attempt to solve it only to give up in despair. This, in a nutshell, is how many Palestinians view Israeli political attitudes toward resolving the conflict.

Recognition of the reality of the state of Israel and its continued existence has been a major psychological hurdle for the Palestinians. There is no doubt in my mind that we have largely and successfully overcome this hurdle, not out of love for the Israelis but as a result of the final recognition of finding realistic grounds to maintain our national identity. I believe the Israelis have not overcome their hurdle yet: the hurdle of finally recognizing the Palestinians as a nation willing to coexist with all others on part of their former Palestine. It is also the hurdle that would take them away from the illusion that it is only a question of time and perseverance—and the Palestinians as a nation will vanish.

To my mind initiating and maintaining dialogue between Palestinians and Israelis is not the obstacle. The obstacle lies in shedding negative fears and preconceived notions that do not relate to realities. In this respect dialogue and other forms of constructive contact can be supremely useful. Palestinians have achieved much in shedding their fears. By doing so, they have gained a lot of additional confidence, which allows them to embark on crossing what are to them much smaller hurdles like dialogue and negotiations. Israelis still have a long way to go in the direction of recognizing the circle for what it is and abandoning the illusions of squaring it. Their success or failure is very much a Palestinian concern.

(I am indebted to my friend Dr. M. A. Alami for his help in the English formulation of my views. His comments and views, though not fully identical with mine, are also appreciated.)

10

The Learning and Teaching of Dialogue: Obstacles and Helps

Mariam Mar'i

My most important lesson in dialogue occurred on the afternoon following the night that my husband, Sami, was arrested. Sami was released after less than twenty-four hours due to the immediate intervention on his behalf of many of our Jewish friends. He was never charged with any wrongdoing. On that afternoon two of those close friends came to our house. I was alone and tense, wanting to believe that Sami would soon be released. One of the friends was especially inquisitive as to the manner of Sami's arrest.

"Tell me in detail, Mariam, how was he arrested?" he requested.

"There is not much to say," I responded in a shivering voice. "It was after midnight. I was already in bed; Sami was in the kitchen getting something to eat or drink. Suddenly the doorbell rang. It was strange that at such an hour somebody should ring, so I got up. I met Sami in the living room and asked him who it could be. He shrugged his shoulders and we both walked over to the door and looked out through the eyehole. That was when we saw the police. They were waiting quietly for us to open the door."

"What did you do?" he asked.

"Before we had a chance to do something, they began to ring again, this time they accompanied it with strong banging on the door. Sami walked quickly to the door and opened it."

"Why?"

"Well ... probably because we were ashamed to have the police waiting outside our door. We didn't want the neighbors to see them."

"That was your mistake!" he cried. "Why did *you* feel ashamed? The police knew they were arresting an innocent man. *They* should have been ashamed. By coming after midnight they shifted the shame onto you. Your mistake is exactly the mistake the Jews, my relatives, made when they were being rounded up by the Gestapo in Germany. They were ashamed to cry out, to scream that injustice was being done. You should have made the police knock until they woke up all your neighbors, you should have made them aware that you know that they are guilty of an injustice. Instead you shifted the burden of guilt onto your own shoulders."

He was so right that I was overwhelmed. I then vowed never to allow anyone—the establishment, the police, Jewish citizens of Israel—to make me feel guilty when I knew that I was innocent. When Sami died of a heart attack a year later, I renewed my vow, because I knew that I must now struggle alone.

I call this incident my most important lesson in dialogue because Jews often attempt to make us Israeli Arabs feel guilty for our aspirations, for our beliefs, for our mere existence. If we accept this guilt, it will not allow us to confront Jews in dialogue, to live with them as partners in this area of the world. In other words, for us Israeli Arabs striving for dialogue is a daily struggle, often an ugly struggle. Before elaborating upon these struggles, let me say a bit about my philosophy of dialogue.

During my graduate studies my understanding of dialogue was very much influenced by Paulo Freire, the Brazilian educator whose writings, I felt, spoke directly to my way of life and thoughts. I sensed that I had lived through much of what Freire had formulated. With me, as Freire noted, consciousness of my situation was a result of learning and of my being involved in changing that situation; and I could only change that situation by relating dialogically to those persons who viewed such changes with fear and apprehension. All this sounds too simple or perhaps very abstract; so let me give a seemingly simple example—my struggle twenty-five years ago, as an Arab Muslim female teenager, to attain a university degree. (Perhaps the difficulties of this struggle will be understood if I mention that today, in 1989, one finds in Israel only three Israeli Arab women, among them myself, who have earned a Ph.D.)

My father was seventy-four years old when I was born. My mother was his fourth wife. I was his youngest child, and I had little direct contact with him. When I reached the tenth grade, my father notified my mother and myself that this would be my last year in school. He felt that there was no sense for a girl to study, since her natural place was the home. I was determined to continue my studies; I already dreamed of studying at a university. But I felt that rebelling directly against my father would be futile. At that early age I sensed that I must change his way of thinking, his viewing me as a woman whose only role is in the home. Freire would have said that I must change his manner of reflecting upon the world and his place in it.

I spoke to my brother and sister; they expressed sympathy with my desire to continue my education, but I did not sense that they were willing to confront my father. I should add here that some of my brothers from my father's previous marriages, including my father's oldest son, were refugees in Lebanon. They became refugees as a result of the 1948 Israeli-Arab war when they fled from our hometown, Acre. After the creation of the state of Israel, they were never allowed to return. I decided to write to this older brother whom I had never met, except when I was a baby, and ask him to intervene on my behalf. My letter was sent to Turkey and from there to Lebanon, since there was and still is no direct mail service between Lebanon and Israel. An answer soon arrived. That brother explained to my father that in the volatile and insecure political situation in the Middle East, it would be wise to have women with academic knowledge, so that they can find a job when needed.

My father read the letter carefully and then summoned the entire family. He was already ninety years old. He notified everyone that from now on, the eldest of my brothers living with us would be in charge of decisions such as whether I would continue my studies. He explained that the world had changed so much since he had matured that he feared to make a decision that might be wrong and cause undue suffering. In short, my ninety-year-old father had learned something from the entire incident. I felt that in this manner of dealing with my wish to study, I had helped my family learn to accept my freedom and perhaps to appreciate it.

That teenage incident seems to have influenced much of my personal development. It may have been at the basis of my wish to initiate change in my Israeli-Arab milieu while ensuring that this change would not threaten many of my fellow Arabs or their ingrained traditional values and way of life. I suspect that it has encouraged me to believe in dialogue and to work for Jewish-Arab dialogue. I have often confronted both my fellow Jews and my fellow Arabs and requested that they involve themselves in changing our oppressive situation. Again and again I have encouraged persons to change their perceptions by personally rejecting oppression and by relating dialogically to each other.

As I read the above paragraph, it all sounds naive. Seemingly, one just has to be dialogical and everything will work out. That is a mistake. It never was easy, and it is not now.

Freire believes that genuine dialogue occurs when two persons are open to each other and, by speaking truthfully, are willing to change the meaning of their shared world — as he puts it, "to speak a true word is to transform the world."[1] I may be naive but I am willing to speak to every person, including Jewish fanatics such as Meir Kahane who wish to evict us Arabs from this land, even though we are citizens and have resided here for generations before he came to the land. I believe that if we will be open to each other and speak truthfully, we may be able to transform the hatred that encompasses us into an understanding and acceptance of each other. And my personal experience supports this belief. I have reached dialogical relations with Jewish women; we grew up in different, rather hostile, societies, yet our belief in dialogue helped us become friends. Now our different backgrounds often add spice to our relationships.

Again I am writing as if it is too easy. My problem is, as a psychologist friend told me, that I do not know how to scream. Somewhere in my youth or childhood that ability to scream was smothered. Even when Sami died, I could not scream, I could not wail. The only time I remember myself screaming suddenly was in a public lecture I was giving, when someone asked me what I would do if the Jews suddenly started evicting all Arabs from Israel. I got up to answer and found myself screaming that I would struggle like a wild animal who has been attacked. My not screaming is bad, because I know that at times the truth only emerges in a scream.

But I am not myopic. I know that the relations between Jews and Arabs in Israel have not been dialogical for years, and lately the situation has gotten worse. It is terrible; I often hate living in such a situation. It is quite an understatement to say that the response of most Israeli Jews to the Palestinian uprising has been antidialogical. These sons and daughters of Holocaust survivors and of Jews who fled from Arab lands refuse to understand that, like Freire's Brazilian peasants who became conscious of their being exploited and oppressed, the Palestinians in the occupied territories have finally become conscious of their being exploited and oppressed—and they wish to end that situation. And I believe that sooner or later they will bring about the end of the Israeli occupation.

Hence, Jews in Israel must grasp that entering dialogue with Palestinians today requires accepting them as free persons who deserve a space to live their freedom. Translated into political terms, this means that Israel must allow for a neighboring Palestinian state to arise in the occupied territories. Dialogue and oppression can rarely get along together, if at all; hence Israel must terminate the military occupation, and the sooner the better. I also hold that Israel must legislate laws that ensure equality and freedom for all its citizens, including the Israeli Arabs.

Before giving an example of one of my major failures in dialogue, I want to stress that many of the Jewish-Arab dialogue groups that have sprouted and then withered and disappeared during the past four decades in Israel have exploited the Arab participants. In these groups the Arab became an object of interest for the Jew, or at times an object that would help the Jew become sensitive to Arabs. Now, I do not think that this was totally bad, but it was not good for the Arab, and especially if the participant was an Arab teenager. Dialogue can only arise between subjects—that is, between free subjective persons. When one of the persons is set in a situation where he or she is an object of interest for the other, that person does not respond dialogically and does not develop as a person through the encounter. Such is especially true in our situation where the Arabs are an oppressed minority.

In general, in the difficult dialogue encounter between Jewish and Arab teenagers, it is often better when each person comes prepared for what may happen. For instance, the Arab should know that the Jew may merely want to use him or her so as to develop one's own sensitivity. The Arab must then not fear to unmask these intentions, because only then can one reach genuine dialogue. Or, as I put it at times, dialogue is often born out of pain. In other words, like the peasants whom Freire educated, our Arab teenagers must understand that they have the right to struggle, they have the right to demand that Jews relate to them as equals, as persons with freedom and dignity. Furthermore, the Arabs must learn to trust in themselves and to be proud of themselves as Arabs and as Palestinians. They should learn to appreciate, perhaps even to cherish, their heritage, including their religious heritage, be it Christian or Muslim. When they attain this pride, when they know that they have the right to struggle for freedom, when they are conscious of themselves as proud struggling persons, they can involve themselves as equals in any meeting with Jews. Such an involvement of persons who can contribute of their freedom to the dialogical encounter, which may or may not emerge, has been one of my goals as an educator for dialogue.

I wish the situation in Israel could justify my belief in dialogue. It does not. In the past few years the right-wing Jewish parties are spreading hatred of Arabs and are working to erode the democratic principles upon which Israeli society is supposedly established. Slowly they are succeeding in intimidating some Knesset members of left-wing parties and in converting to their blatant jingoism and racism many of the persons who formerly believed in equal rights for Arabs. I suspect that my recent major failure in dialogue, which has perturbed me lately, should be viewed against the background of these developments. Here is the story.

Recently Mr. Dan Meridor, the right-wing minister of justice, proposed an amendment to the 1948 Prevention of Terrorism Act; the role of the amendment is to limit and possibly eradicate all volunteer Arab institutions and organizations in Israel. These institutions and organizations receive much, perhaps 90 percent, of their funding, millions of dollars, from charitable organizations in the United States and Western Europe. The amendment would make it a crime to receive funds or property knowingly or unknowingly from a "terrorist" organization. One should add that no one has to prove that some organizations are terrorist. If a government official decides that such an organization is "terrorist," this decision cannot be challenged in court. Such funds or property can be seized by the police if there is what the amendment calls "reasonable suspicion." The police would not need a search warrant or an order signed by a judge. I should add that the reasons the police would confiscate the funds from an institution or organization do not have to be presented in court to the person whose property was confiscated, because under security laws it can be deemed evidence that cannot be disclosed. In short, the police can come one night, like the night they came to take my husband, Sami—but now it will be worse—they can come and take all my property and never be required to explain in court the reasons for their actions. And all this under the facade of a democratic regime!

One might wonder why I, a person who deals with educating kindergarten and nursery school teachers, should have to worry about such a law. Consider what Mr. Dan Meridor said in an interview about the law to the newspaper *Kol Ha'ir*: "If I know that this [allegedly "terrorist"] organization donates money to nurseries in order that in the future these children will go out and riot, should I be naive and close my eyes?" When I read that statement I wondered: how paranoid Mr. Meridor must be if he views Arab nursery children, aged three to five, as prospective enemies and is already setting up laws to deny them education.

It should be added that government funding for most Arab schools and other public institutions and organizations may at times be only one-third of what similar Jewish public institutions and organizations receive. Hence the Arabs set up volunteer, philanthropy-funded institutions and organizations that fulfill the roles of public institutions and organizations in the Jewish sector. Consequently, the proposed law will now threaten the existence of all these volunteer institutions. But more important to my mind, as an Arab woman who learned to live in Israel and to cherish the democratic way of life, this law undermines the democratic regime that currently prevails.

Here is where my failure in dialogue occurred. Representatives of some eighty volunteer organizations met and chose a committee of three people, among them myself, to represent them in a meeting with the Knesset Legislation Committee that was to discuss, accept, or challenge the law. We met with the Knesset committee and spoke with them an hour and a half explaining at length how the proposed amendment to the Prevention of Terrorism Act was eroding Israeli democracy and making Israel into a police state. At first some Knesset members tried to make us feel guilty that we were challenging the law, but I remembered my lesson from Sami's arrest, and I tried to make them feel ashamed that they had proposed such a law. We sat with them for an hour and a half, we felt that our arguments were valid, and more important we felt that Knesset members were listening to our arguments. We left believing we had made our point.

We were wrong. There was no dialogue in that meeting, only a polite accommodation of our views. A week later we learned that the chairman of the committee, who had promised us to discuss in depth with members of the committee each article of the amendment so that our concerns would be met—this same chairman rushed the articles through the committee, voting on them without discussion. His manner of approving the law was in such contrast to accepted procedure that the amendment was returned to the committee for a renewed review. Unfortunately, the draconian amendment will probably soon be approved.

Despite such deep disappointments I can only say that I will continue to struggle for dialogue, for understanding, for democracy, for human rights. I know that we Arabs are oppressed in Israel, and that those Israelis who oppress us are doing wrong. But again and again I am inspired by Freire's saying, "It is only the oppressed, who by freeing themselves, can free their oppressors."[2]

NOTES

1. Paulo Freire, *Pedagogy of the Oppressed* (New York: Continuum, 1970), p. 75.

2. Ibid., p. 42.

SECTION 6

DIALOGUE AND INTEGRITY

The Gaza Strip seems often to be one of the internationally forgotten areas of human suffering. Recently, the Israeli army started constructing a second tall barbed-wire fence around the entire Gaza Strip, fully closing off this area. Evidently the military authorities believe that the first eight-foot fence topped by barbed-wire concertinas is not enough of a deterrent. Only three well-guarded entrances into Israel allow for traffic back and forth. The seven hundred thousand Palestinians who now live in this area have the dubious honor of living in the largest ghetto in the world. One should also keep in mind what we have already mentioned, that according to U.N. statistics the Gaza Strip is the most densely populated area on earth.

Populated mainly by refugees, two out of every three residents of the area live in shacks, most of them on the verge of poverty, and are recognized as citizens of no country. It is a small wonder that the Palestinian uprising began, as Zvi Gilat describes it, in the Gaza Strip. The refugee population, and especially the younger population, suddenly understood that under the harsh Israeli military rule, their bodies often racked by the ongoing economic exploitation, they had nothing left to lose. Nothing, that is, except their integrity.

That is the reason they arose with stones in their hands and demanded a change. Immediately. That is the reason they continue month after month after month to throw stones at Israeli vehicles, to march, to unfurl Palestinian flags, despite the rise

147

in the number of casualties, despite their being hauled off to jail, beaten brutally, persecuted mentally, and finally condemned in a farcical military trial to months or years of incarceration. And they won. Today, these young refugees proudly show off their wounds, proudly continue their daily struggle, proudly believe in their quest for freedom. And suddenly, many of them are willing to be partners in dialogue—if it is dialogue among equals, at eye level, as Zvi Gilat calls it.

If it is the younger generation of refugees who, with rocks in their hands, enthusiastically rediscovered Palestinian integrity, it is the older generation of indigenous Palestinians who stubbornly kept the flame of Palestinian integrity alive during the long years of oppression and persecution. (Not only under Israeli rule. The Egyptians also oppressed, exploited, and persecuted the Palestinians in Gaza when they ruled the area.) Prominent among these indigenous Palestinians is Haidar Abdel Shafi, a retired medical doctor who is chairman of the Red Crescent Society in Gaza. As he shows in his essay, guarding his integrity was no simple task in such a situation of continuous oppression. He did it with fortitude.

Such fortitude is one of the aspects that attracted Zvi Gilat, a journalist for the Israeli daily newspaper *Hadoshot*, to the Palestinian uprising. He found such fortitude daily among the Palestinians whom he met while covering the rapid development of the *intifada*. He also found their rediscovered Palestinian integrity: in the joyful eyes of the young teenaged rock-throwing, flag-waving Palestinians, in the measured, careful responses of their parents and leaders. And with this reborn integrity came a new willingness to relate wholly to Israelis, to see the quest for dialogue as a mutual quest, a way to go beyond the oppression, hostility, and violence that currently prevail.

11

Integrity and Dialogue:
My Reasons for Skepticism

HAIDAR ABDEL SHAFI

I am not a great believer in the possibility of Israeli-Palestinian dialogue right now, even though I have participated in a few dialogue events—or happenings, if you like. Perhaps my skepticism stems from the feeling that for more than two decades the Israelis have been attempting to eradicate our integrity, as a people, as a community, and as persons. In that process, ironically, many Israelis have also lost much of their own self-respect. Without mutual respect, I doubt that dialogue can emerge. Looking back on my personal history, I feel that it need not have been so.

I was born in Gaza in 1919 and received my secondary education in the Arab college in Jerusalem after which I enrolled in the American University in Beirut and graduated as a medical doctor in 1943. I worked for a short while in the government hospital in Jaffa and there I had the opportunity to meet Jewish nurses and doctors. But my first meetings with Jews were much earlier.

In the middle 1920s my father, who was a religious man, was appointed the custodian of Islamic property in Hebron. During that period we lived in Hebron. Opposite the door of our apartment was a flat in which a Jewish family lived. Every Saturday morning the Jewish lady would come and knock at our door and call me by name to come into their apartment and put out the kerosene lamps. What is more, the Jewish rabbi used to visit my father; sometimes his daughter would accompany him. Down in the street opposite our building there was a Jewish grocery and it seemed normal to buy from them. Thus the relations with Jews that I experienced as a child did not leave in my mind any impression of problems between Jews and Arabs. There was mutual respect despite the differences. We stayed in Hebron for two years. It was very troubling for me when I heard about the Arab massacres of Jews in Hebron in 1929, which took place after we were back in Gaza. Then I started to know and to become aware of the Zionist movement.

I also had some association with Jews when I studied in the American University in Beirut. There were several Jewish students at the university, some of them were from Palestine and some from abroad. I did not have much contact with them; most of them seemed to me emotional and provocative, but one of them became my best friend. I knew that he settled in Israel and I looked for him after 1967, when we could again visit Israel, but I could not find him. He had married a Jewish girl from Lebanon.

During the period I worked in the government hospital in Jaffa I was also introduced to some Jewish friends in Tel Aviv by Arab friends of mine in Jaffa. That was when we had chances for discussions, but the dialogue at that time was mostly about what was going on. There was the pressing problem of Jewish refugees who had fled Hitler's murderers, there were the expectations of what could happen after the Second World War. That was what we discussed. With the knowledge of the Nazi atrocities spreading, our Jewish friends were pressing us to support emigration of Jews to Israel, because their situation was pressing. I do not remember the outcomes of all of these discussions, but I do recall that there was mutual agreement between us that we were striving for a democratic secular Jewish and Arab Palestinian state. After the 1947 war and after the Arab refugee problem came about, it seemed to me that Jewish people — I mean those who had agreed with us to establish a bilateral secular state — either they were not sincere or the point of view of the Zionist leadership was so overwhelming that they had no chance to struggle for the realization of their point of view. To me this was a discouraging experience. It also helped make me skeptical about dialogue.

In 1945 I came to Gaza and set up a private practice. I had wished to enroll for postgraduate studies, but events moved quickly and I was in Gaza in 1948 when the war took place and I witnessed the exodus of the Palestinian refugees. In late 1949 I left for the United States to do postgraduate studies. I was away until mid-1954 when I returned and settled in Gaza, continuing in my private medical practice. During the occupation of 1956 there was no chance of meeting Jews who were not part of the military authority. Since the occupation of 1967 we have been in contact with Jews and have had conversations with them. Yet within a situation of occupation, I must say that I myself had no personal initiative for dialogue.

Over the years I undertook political roles in which I could help my people reestablish their identity. In the 1950s I was nominated by the Egyptian administration to be director of medical services, which I did for three years, after which I resigned. In 1961 the Egyptians established a national union for the area of Gaza. I stood for elections for it and was elected. In 1962 they established a legislative council and I was elected to the legislative council. At the first meeting I was elected the speaker of the council for the term of a year and I was reelected in 1963. In May 1964 I participated in the meeting of the Palestinian National Council that met in East Jerusalem as a member of the delegation from Gaza, which included fifty people. I was nominated to be a member of the PLO executive, which I did for one year, living most of the time in Jerusalem. After that I returned to Gaza to work again as a private physician and was in Gaza when the Israeli occupation took place in 1967.

Perhaps the most telling example of the cynicism of Israeli authorities — and everyone knows how difficult it is to dialogue with a cynic — has to do with our attempts to set up a branch of the Red Crescent in Gaza. After the occupation some people in my age group got together and were wondering what they could do to help their fellow Palestinians, not only medically but also spiritually. A few of us set up a founding committee to establish the Red Crescent Society of Gaza. It took over a year to get a permit from the military authorities to formally establish the society. Finally, they gave us the permit in June 1969, but two weeks later they froze the permit. They said we were not allowed to engage in any activities, and did not give any explanation. At that time I was exiled to Sinai with two other residents of Gaza, to Nachel, a military post in the middle of the desert with only Bedouin tribes around it. After three months I returned, but the Red Crescent Society remained frozen for almost three years. Thanks to one of our members talking with Defense Minister Moshe Dayan, it was finally allowed to operate.

I have never tried to conceal from the authorities my criticism of the Israeli occupation. They responded by administrative measures. When they allowed the Red Crescent to operate, we were not able to start our activities right away. From the beginning the authorities tried to interfere. They alleged that our administrative committee, composed of fifteen persons, was not adequate or representative.

I realized that they wanted to name someone to be on the administrative committee. My response was: "Sorry, it might be true that there is not adequate representation, but this is a voluntary secular organization. It does not need to be representative." And I added "I have no objection to adding persons to our administrative committee, but changes must come through the constitution, and our constitution stipulates an administrative committee of fifteen persons and we have fifteen persons already on the committee. For the moment therefore we cannot fulfill your desire. We have to wait for our yearly meeting to convene and change the constitution so that twenty-one members can be on the administrative committee."

We argued for six months without being able to start our activities. Finally they got tired and allowed us to begin our work, but I knew that we were in disfavor.

Indeed almost immediately the Israel Security Service started a process of incitement against the Red Crescent Society. I knew that because people who were summoned by the military for interrogation came to me again and again and told me that in the course of their interrogation they were asked repeatedly about the activities of the Red Crescent. They started by alleging that we were PLO, that we were a political organization, then they changed their tune and said that we were Fatah, and finally they decided to call us communists.

The Israelis also used a policy of divide and conquer against those of us who were influential in the Red Crescent Society. After the emergence of the Muslim fundamentalist movement, they stressed the fact that in the Red Crescent Society we were described as communists. The result was some tension between us and the fundamentalist movement, especially from their side. Personally, I kept a very objective attitude and never openly criticized the Muslim fundamentalists. I always advocated that we must follow principles of dialogue, of free discussion. But they rejected these principles and denounced me, while I was trying to promote a new attitude toward the role of women. Later they went further. In January 1980 the premises of the Red Crescent Society were ransacked by fundamentalists; they also burned our library. While all this was occurring, the Israeli military authorities placidly looked on. That was a very shameful act. It was really a tragedy. It is unbelievable that anybody could burn a general library. In spite of that I have attempted to be flexible; I even pretended that the fundamentalists did this in a moment of absentmindedness. I asked them to meet with us and speak in open dialogue. But they always refrained from meeting with us in open dialogue. They are not ready for it. It seems that wherever you invoke God as justifying your extreme aggressive actions, there is no more dialogue.

As I look back on the continual trampling of our integrity, I repeatedly wonder why the Israeli authorities did not permit us to pursue all the activities of educating our people. From the beginning the Red Crescent Society was active in some cultural fields, aside from our work in the medical field. We organized book exhibits, art exhibits, folklore festivals, and we arranged for a series of lectures for the public on various topics — all these activities were open for both men and women. Some of these lectures dealt with the role of women. Once after we had such a lecture dealing with women, on the next day we were opposed from the rostrum of the mosque. Still, our lectures met with an unexpected appreciation by the public. That may be the reason why in 1978 the Israeli authorities clamped down on our cultural activities. Once we had already organized a lecture and had convened at the time that the lecture was going to take place; suddenly I saw that the military governor was present; he notified us all to go home. He gave no reason for his decision. After that the military authorities simply sealed off all our activities.

I spoke to the representatives of the International Red Cross about the canceling of our lecture series. They were perturbed. I suggested a test case: "Let us approach the authorities with the idea that I asked you people to give us a lecture on the workings of the International Red Cross around the world. Let's see what their response will be." We sent a request to organize such a lecture to the authorities. Permission was denied.

When I mention the cynicism of the Israeli authorities as hindering dialogue, it brings back some vivid personal recollections. In 1970 the Israeli authorities deported me to Lebanon together with another person from Gaza and four people from the West Bank. It was a cruel manner of trampling upon our freedom and human rights.

In September 1970 I was summoned by the military governor of Gaza and when I entered his office he said to me very abruptly: "For how long are you Arabs going to continue behaving like this?"

I was taken aback and asked: "What are you talking about?"

During those days three planes had been hijacked to Jordan by members of the PLO. The military governor surprised me and retorted: "I am talking about the planes."

I asked: "What can I do about it?"

He said: "Why don't you go out and speak to George Habash?"

I was surprised at this soldier and said: "Well, if you think that I am an advisor to George Habash, I am not. And if President Nasser cannot prevail on George Habash, I don't think that I can really help."

That was the end of the meeting, which did not last more than five minutes and I left angry at him. That night in the middle of the night the army police came to my house and asked me to go with them. I was taken to a prison. When I was there, they brought the other fellow who was to be deported with me, the ex-mayor of Gaza. As I was being taken to prison, I was wondering what this was all about. And when I saw my fellow prisoner I wondered even more, since I had no close association with him.

They kept us together in a cell. We talked all night, wondering about the reasons for our incarceration. In the morning an officer came and said: "You are going to be deported." I was very worried at the beginning because I knew that my fellow prisoner had some chronic illnesses. I was afraid that they would put us across the Jordanian border, in the middle of the desert, and it would be difficult for him to survive. But once we passed Ashkelon and continued north, I felt that it would be all right, since we would probably be deported to Lebanon. They took us to a military post on the Lebanese border in the middle of the Galilee, and there we waited for quite a period. We did not know why. Later they put us into a car and convoy, and we drove to the border. Only when we reached the fence, we learned that four other Palestinians from the West Bank were being deported with us. They put us across the fence and told us to keep going into Lebanon and not to turn back.

We were the only deportees who were permitted to return. We were deported on September 12. A week later there was a confrontation between the PLO and the Jordanian army. When the PLO was routed — this is my personal explanation — I think the military Israelis were very euphoric and happy with this development, so they were willing to allow us to return. In addition, I should mention that the Red Cross was demanding to get us back, especially because there was no reason for this deportation. Finally, the Israelis asked that our families put in an application for family reunion, and that was what we did, and it came as a pleasant surprise. But the entire experience hardly encouraged me to believe in dialogue with Israelis. I want to stress that the permission to return was not a retraction of their act.

Despite my skepticism, despite my being in disfavor, whenever the opportunity arose for me to state my views, including when there were visitors, I did not hesitate to speak straight-forwardly. I repeatedly stated that the Palestinians are the indig-enous people of the land, and if they should concede some rights for the Israelis in Palestinian territory on the basis of existing facts, there should be no question of their own rights, which are innate and inalienable. For instance, when the autonomy con-cept was suggested, I was against it. First, because it denies us Palestinians our basic political and civil rights. Second, when I heard about Begin's views of autonomy, I was much more deter-mined to reject this proposal. I am quite sure that my straight-forwardness raised doubts in the authorities' minds that I could be involved in the Red Crescent Society merely for charitable or educational reasons.

Although I never initiated any process for dialogue, I was ready to be involved in dialogue. For instance, when I was called upon to participate in the New Outlook seminar that was arranged for moderate Jews and Palestinians in September 1978, I participated. The impression I got from this two-day seminar was hardly encouraging. It seems to me that if dialogue is to be productive, if it is to lead to an enhanced situation, certain pre-conditions must be met. I do not think one can involve oneself in a positive dialogue if one does not rid oneself of all kinds of prejudices. One must come to the dialogue with a truly receptive mind. For me dialogue is a means to explore issues, whether abstract and general or particular and special. I also think that dialogue should aim at establishing principles. In this it differs from negotiation. Negotiation is a means of reaching agreement. But before negotiations start, I believe that dialogue has to establish principles. And unless you rid yourself of certain prej-udices from the beginning, from key phrases that obsess your mind, I do not think anybody can be involved in substantive dialogue.

In the New Outlook seminar, which was attended by promi-nent Israelis, many of them university professors, journalists, and active politicians, it seemed to me that the main difficulty was in two areas. The first was the difficulty of our Israeli coun-terparts to assess and to evaluate the Palestinian position. This was partially a result of an overemphasis of Israeli fear and duress. Second, I thought that the fact that Israel has a far superior state—militarily and organizationally—than the Palestinians, certainly should allow Israelis to rid themselves of complexes. When you rid yourself of complexes, it means that you put yourself in a position equal to the person you are encountering; then the process of dialogue can emerge. I cannot establish dialogue with anyone who is not in an equal situation.

I cannot say that the responses of Israelis differed in other dialogues in which I participated: in the United States, Nightline with Ted Koppel, and a similar meeting on BBC television.

Let me be blunt. My criticism of the Israelis in these so-called dialogical meetings is that they lack the ability to size up the Palestinian position. I have met no less than seven times in so-called dialogical encounters with Israelis, and not only with political figures; for instance, I met with Jews from Eastern European countries, professors, journalists, artists, critics—and always there was difficulty in reaching discussion of principles because the Israelis were unable to get rid of initial prejudices. Let me give a specific example. If I want to negotiate for peace, I want the Israeli side to appreciate my position as a Palestinian. Now, any appreciation of my position cannot ignore two basic matters: the question of my right for a state on Palestinian soil and the question of the Palestinian refugees. Irrespective of the complexities that these questions bring up, when one wants to deal specifically with these matters, I expect a sincere Israeli who wants to have dialogue with authentic Palestinians to appreciate my situation. Most of these Israelis whom I met, and who are from the left and from the peace movement, whenever I put up the question that we Palestinians cannot close our eyes to the problems of the refugees, their consistent response is, and sometimes it comes off just like that, like the raising of a red flag: no, you cannot bring this up as a matter of discussion.

How can I as a Palestinian—and I know that the United Nations has decisions about the refugees, and I know that Israel firmly refuses to allow one refugee to return into the area of Israel proper—with all that knowledge how can I as a Palestinian ignore, neglect, and forget the problem of the refugees? I cannot! If I respect myself this problem must figure in any process of negotiations that I have with the Israelis. And I say negotiations. I am not saying that a solution should be imposed upon

Israel, even though it is true that the U.N. resolution says that the refugees should have the option of going back to their homes or being compensated.

Of course we have red-flag people on the Palestinian side also. There is a Palestinian minority who is convinced as to the abstract absolute right of the Palestinian people to hold the whole territory of Palestine. In the resolutions of the Palestinian National Council (PNC) it became clear that the majority do not believe in the practicality of these views. It is of course important to say that the acceptance of the Jewish state by the Palestinian people and the PNC did not come about spontaneously. It required a period of sincere dialogue within Palestinian society itself. Hence, I believe that a dialogue within Israeli society must precede dialogue with the Palestinians. This inner Israeli dialogue must be geared toward respecting the integrity of the Palestinian people; from such an approach will emerge a proper position toward the Palestinians.

To tell the truth, the resolutions of the PNC advocating peace and calling for dialogue with Israel came as a surprise to many of our people. But discussions about these issues had been discreetly conducted within the occupied territories for quite a while and a quite general consensus was reached about the importance of adopting these positions, and it was conveyed to Palestinians outside Israel.

I am advocating the need to restore our integrity, because it is sneered upon and derided every day by Israelis. When I speak to the military authorities about my views on the need to establish a Palestinian state and our need to live together peacefully as neighbors, they dismiss me with derision, calling me a dreamer. When I wanted to travel abroad to visit my children in Europe, I met the coordinator of the territories, a general whom I had never met before. The moment I met him we shook hands and he said: "Are you going to be like always, not accepting and then regretting that after ten years?" That was his first statement to me. I told him, "I think that you are the party who is going to regret, since you are offered a unique opportunity for peace with the Palestinians." The attitude of this general was the arrogance of a person in a position of strength who shows no respect for fellow inhabitants of this area. I do not know how many Israelis act like this, but their position is one of strength based on military force alone. It is not the strength of democratic principles accepted by the United Nations.

I am stressing the importance of personal integrity because I want the future Palestinian state to be democratic and pluralistic. I do not think that we have any other alternative. I suspect that it will be the first Arab democratic state. I think that the majority of Palestinians, including myself, would choose such a state. We not only appreciate democracy as a principle that ensures personal freedom and dignity, but from a practical point of view I think that only a democratic way of life can help us meet the legion of problems that we are going to face as a state. Only by democratic means can we hope to resolve the conflicts between the different ideologies within the Palestinian people.

I cannot pretend that we are perfect. We have many failings and faults that need to be rectified. It will not be easy. We have made mistakes during the *intifada*, for instance, when the *intifada* leadership took the Israeli-issued magnetic cards away from those workers who were pressed to take magnetic cards in order to make a living. Later they realized that it was a mistake, as they failed to provide any alternative.

In closing let me make one suggestion to any Israeli who is speaking to me in dialogue: when you are faced with an issue in the confrontation between us, do not limit your thinking to the specifics of that issue, but make an honest attempt to see everything in a much broader context. Make the attempt to look far out into the future. And while you are looking, try to remember that whatever is being done today is going to leave effects on future generations. I believe that through mutual respect and dialogue, we can make that future better.

12

Dialogue Is Possible
Only at Eye Level:
Intifada and an
Israeli Journalist

Zvi Gilat

My reporting on the *intifada* for my newspaper *Hadoshot* began almost by accident, but I was immediately swept away by the pace and the power of the events. Looking back it seems that the *intifada* pulled me into its whirlpool of events already from its first hours. Yet perhaps these hours indicate most clearly both the problematics and the hope of Israeli-Palestinian dialogue that may emerge in the wake of this popular uprising.

A few days before the eruption of the *intifada*, Shimon Peres, leader of the Labor Alliance, threw out one of his seemingly "daring" ideas: to convert the Gaza Strip into a demilitarized zone, a situation that would prevail until we reach a peace settlement with the Palestinians. The idea seemed so unrealistic that I decided to visit the Gaza Strip and to write an ironical report of a supposed tourist who reaches this "newly established demilitarized area" for the first time.

From my work as a reporter I was well acquainted with the Gaza Strip and with many other areas in the occupied territories. Most of the articles I had written before the *intifada* had described the uncalled-for suffering of Palestinians in these areas under the wretched conditions imposed upon them by the Israeli authorities. Quite often I described how these conditions allowed individuals to illegally oppress and exploit Palestinians. In these reports the Palestinian residents of the occupied territories were often depicted as persons in despair, who sadly accepted the cruelties of the occupation, who lacked the hope needed to change their situation for the better. When I met with Palestinian leaders, they were very often hesitant in expressing their views. They spoke about injustice, about the need for democracy, but they often sounded detached from the everyday degrading reality of the Palestinian people's situation.

Accompanied by a photographer I reached the supposedly "newly established demilitarized area" of the Gaza Strip around 9:30 in the morning. As we approached the city of Gaza we saw black smoke bellowing upward from the area near Shifa hospital. Attracted by a possible story, we drove in that direction, and as we approached everything became anarchic, confusing, scary.

Three masked Palestinians stopped the car—they had identified us as Israelis by the yellow license plate—and immediately began banging on the roof. Two of them wanted to block our way and the third tried to make us abandon the car. After a few seconds of arguing, a person who looked like their leader approached and decided to listen to us. We explained that we were reporters working on a story and when we saw the smoke bellowing upward from this area, we decided to come so as to report the incident.

"Jews?" he asked.

"Jews," we answered.

"Then come with me," he said. "And see what Jews are capable of doing."

We were already surrounded by around twenty excited young Palestinians who had been burning tires. I understood that we had lost our freedom and had been taken into custody by these young men. We followed the leader into the hospital.

The scene inside the hospital was very depressing. As we entered, people started bringing in the first casualties from Gebalia refugee camp—these were the first casualties of the *intifada*. The squalor, the wretchedness, the lack of equipment needed to provide the wounded with adequate treatment, the bloodstains on the floor, all this was very depressing and, when I look back now, very irritating.

"Let them photograph and write and tell the entire world!" someone beside me yelled.

Another person grabbed my shirt and yelled: "Look what your people are doing to us! See what your soldiers did! They have no heart! Aren't both of you soldiers, too?"

Excitement was boiling over. Again and again someone would doubt that we were reporters and we would have to show our identity card. Again and again someone would scream at us: "What do you say of this? Is this right?"

Again and again I would answer, exasperated: "If this was right, I wouldn't be here to write about it," knowing that my answer yielded little consolation.

After a while the group that was leading us pulled us outside to hear the shooting close to the hospital. One Palestinian dipped his hand in a pool of blood on the road and waved it at us. Another approached us with a large rock in his hand threatening us until pacified by our guides. When we finally reached our car, we found that all our windows had been smashed in.

"Children did it," someone said with a smile. "They couldn't be stopped."

On the way back to Tel Aviv we saw how Arab youths provoke Israeli soldiers from very close, knowing that they might be shot, but standing there, provoking, throwing stones, as if they had nothing to lose.

The force of events on that day was so powerful, and my impressions so vivid, that I returned to Gaza on the next day. And since I felt that something new was developing here, something I was unacquainted with in the past, I became involved with the *intifada*, trying to cover all its changes as they evolved in Israeli and Palestinian society.

During this period the Palestinians who demonstrated in the streets and alleys, who burned tires and threw rocks, usually assisted me. I understand that for many of them I was no more than a means to convey their message. I was the avenue through which that message would reach the world beyond the sordid poverty-ridden refugee camp. (Still, it was quite clear that most Palestinians preferred foreign reporters.) The adults always understood the importance of the Israeli media, the youth not always. At times I was also the target of the rocks they threw, since as an Israeli they saw me as belonging to the regime that was oppressing them. Perhaps these frustrated youths merely wanted to show off their newly attained power and did not give a damn who was hit. Probably the word "Jew" for many of them was like a red cape before a charging bull. I only know that these rock-throwing young zealots were not always careful, and at times hit their fellow Palestinians.

Almost always one could find an adult who would assist Israeli reporters, who would guide us to our destination, and who would guard us against the rock-throwing youths. Once, in Gaza I wanted to interview a top official. The entire road to his office was blocked by burning tires spaced at distances of one hundred to two hundred yards from each other. When I entered the city a Palestinian agreed to help me reach the person I wished to interview. At every blockade we stopped, he got down, explained that he was bringing a reporter, and received permission to continue. After continuing thus for a while, we reached a blockade guarded by two kids, aged eleven or twelve. They refused to let us pass and even wanted to beat the guide and me with the large boards they held. Only when a few adults who saw what was happening intervened and yelled at them, did they allow us to pass.

Yet, on the basis of my work I must say that Palestinian cooperation was not only a result of their recognizing the reporter as an important means in their struggle for freedom. Cooperation on their part was also a result of what may be called a revolution in their self-consciousness. I often felt that even though the *intifada* brought in its wake physical suffering and economic deprivation, it helped many Palestinians regain their lost honor. Suddenly they were no longer a people who acquiesced in being oppressed and exploited, and the Israelis who oppressed them were no longer on a higher existential rung than they. The rules of the game had changed. Their willingness to sacrifice, to struggle heroically, as they saw it, against the evil performed by Israeli soldiers endowed them with a feeling that they were at least equal to their oppressors. And many of them conveyed to me something similar to the following: since I am no longer inferior to you Israelis, we can speak as equals, and that feeling of equality is what I want you as a reporter and a person to hear.

I believe that this change was necessary for genuine dialogue to emerge. The status or external circumstances of two persons may be different; one of them may be discriminated against. But in order for dialogue to occur, the partners to dialogue must both be endowed with a feeling of equality and of recognition of one's own value. Otherwise any attempt to relate dialogically is counterfeit. Before that first day of the *intifada* in Gaza I had many times heard Palestinians exclaim: "Look what you people are doing to us!" It was usually a cry of suffering, or a response to the feeling of being insulted. But when I heard it on the first day of the *intifada* in Gaza, the same words meant something different. They expressed rage, defiance, and belief in their just cause. The Palestinians who screamed at us that day in Gaza were telling us that we Israelis were no longer better than they, that they were now our equals.

Here is another example. In mid-1988 in a village not far from Genin on the West Bank, I interviewed one of the leaders of the *shabiba*, the youth group who were the infantry of the *intifada*. He had just been released after being detained without trial for half a year in one of the Israeli concentration camps. He met us in his father's house, accompanied by a few of his friends. He quietly described the brutality of his guards and depicted some of the abuses, the tortures, and the insults to which he had been exposed in an Israeli prison. But he also related how he and all other jailed Palestinians organized themselves in prison in learning groups in which they studied languages, discussed the ideology of their struggle, and spoke about national aspirations and values.

When the young former prisoner described the tortures he had undergone, one could sense the rage that his stories aroused among his young friends. But what surprised me was that when the interview ended, everyone remained sitting and a few of the

Palestinian youths started to interview me about my stance concerning the situation of the left-wing parties in Israel, including their ability to influence the political developments in the current conflict. They also wanted to know how I viewed the possible outcomes of the *intifada*. These youths, who a few moments ago were depressed and angry at the torture their friend had undergone, felt that now, because of the dangers they daily faced as active supporters of the *intifada*, they could engage in dialogue with any Israeli about the political situation. They were proud of themselves; they knew that they were not inferior to me, and that they could steer the conversation to what concerned them.

I have already mentioned the fact that reporting about the *intifada* could be dangerous, especially for an Israeli reporter. The Palestinians usually felt more comfortable with reporters from abroad, who could usually identify directly with their difficult situation. Often these reporters received more assistance from the Palestinian people. At times when visiting a refugee camp, my Palestinian guide would ask me to speak only English with him and not to notify the people that I worked for an Israeli newspaper. I refused, although I know that some Israeli reporters accepted this advice. I always explained that I am a Jew and work for an Israeli newspaper. I never suffered for this stance. I believe that because I trusted these Palestinians, they trusted me. Of course there were usually two or three minutes of suspicion, but then the interviewer would accept me for what I am.

While reporting from the occupied territories one can often be overcome by the feeling that one is a prisoner of the Palestinians. One often passes by groups of youths with rocks in their hands who might choose you as a target; in many respects they rule the alleys when Israeli army patrols are not around. In such a situation one must not become prisoner of one's own fears and lies, because this fear will block all possibilities of a spontaneous straightforward dialogue.

Perhaps I have described everything as much too simple. During the *intifada* dialogue between an Israeli and a Palestinian is extremely difficult. For me as a reporter, the Palestinian is an object about which I want to report. I am for him also an object, a means in his struggle for freedom, or, at times, a nuisance. But the more each of us gives of ourselves to the conversation and allows one's own doubts and frustrations to emerge, the possibility for sincere conversation grows.

There is also another problem that I have not yet mentioned, my identity as an Israeli. After all, I am an Israeli reporter; it is my army that is doing the oppressing I am describing and criticizing, and this army is doing it in my name. Furthermore, since I also serve in the reserves as does every Israeli, I feel intimate and at home with those fatigue-wearing Israeli soldiers whom I meet. They wear the same clothes I wear when I am called up for duty, they serve in my army.

I suffer from this identity because the Israeli public does not want to see the ugly portrait of itself that emerges from my reporting on the *intifada*. And this is even more true of the soldiers who are serving in the occupied territories. Frequently they express downright hatred of the representatives of the media: "Why do you publish all this about us? You are supporting our enemies, who hate Israel! Are you for us or against us?"

Quite a few times I was attacked violently by Israeli soldiers, and the photographers who accompanied me at times got into fistfights when a soldier tried to interfere with their work or break their camera. In such instances, I would try to explain quietly and soberly something like the following:

"I'm an Israeli as you are. I serve in the army as you do, and I'm no less patriotic than you are. And because of all this I am firmly against what you are doing. You, in your deeds, are providing ammunition to those others whom you fear, to those who hate Israel."

Unfortunately, there are reporters who prefer to work with the army, who show the soldiers that they support their deeds, who thus gain the trust of the army staff. I believe that these reporters are presenting lies. I also believe that such reporting is bad for the army, because among the Israeli soldiers there are many who feel as I do about the situation, and whose need to sincerely relate to a reporter what they know about our army's terrible deeds is no less urgent than my wish to report these deeds.

On one of my visits to Gaza I encountered a crowd of around fifty Palestinians sitting in the square in front of the civil administration building. They sat there silent and angry. Many had been waiting there for days. They had no inkling why. All of them had the same story. A soldier took the person's identity card and told him or her to come to the civil administration building to pick it up. Most of them waited in the square a whole day until finally someone came out and told them to come tomorrow. On the morrow quite often the same thing happened. During each day some were taken to be interrogated or to be incarcerated, most were told to come back the next day, and a few received their identity cards. They sat there the entire day, immersed in fear, or despair, or depression, or apathy.

Yet they were willing to talk. Some spoke in anger, others with a vision that led us both to realms way beyond this depressing reality we shared.

"Together we can create here in the Middle East a wonderful life." A man whom I had never met suddenly spoke up. "We know all about you Israelis, and you know all about us. What concerns us is a home, a family, raising our kids. Do you have children?"

And he was ready to start speaking about the problems that personally concerned us. But that is not the point I wanted to make — that moments of relating personally can emerge, which allow us to discard all formalities and reach out to another person — that such opportunities exist and we only need the courage to respond to them.

No, I wanted to make another point. When we started speaking my interviewee was faced with a choice. Either he spoke to me from down where he was sitting or he stood up. He chose neither. He invited me — an invitation that was more of a demand — to sit down beside him on the dirty pavement. And only when I was seated did he continue speaking.

He was right. Dialogue is possible only when the partners are on the same level, when their eyes are level.

Contributors

Shulamit Aloni is a Knesset member and the head of the Party for Civil Rights and Peace in Israel, which currently has five members in the Israeli Knesset.

Hanan Mikhail-Ashrawi is professor of English literature at Birzeit University. She has been very active in dialogue with Israelis, both in Israel and at international meetings.

Naim Stifan Ateek is canon of St. George's Cathedral in Jerusalem. His recent book is *Justice and Only Justice: A Palestinian Theology of Liberation* (Orbis, 1989).

Zvi Gilat is a journalist for the Israeli daily *Hadoshot*.

Haim Gordon is a senior lecturer at Ben Gurion University in Beer Sheva. Among his books are *Dance, Dialogue, and Despair: Existentialist Philosophy and Education for Peace in Israel* (University of Alabama Press, 1986) and *Education for Peace: Testimonies from World Religions* (Orbis, 1987).

Rivca Gordon works for the Foundation for Democratic Education in Israel.

Faisal Husseini is chairman of the Arab Studies Society in Jerusalem and is currently one of the leading spokesmen for the Palestinians in the West Bank and Gaza.

Zahira Kamal is a leading Palestinian feminist. She is chairwoman of the Palestinian Federation of Women's Action Committees.

Felicia Langer is a leading lawyer who worked for Palestinian rights in Israel. Her latest book on her experiences is *An Age of Stone* (Quartet Books, 1988). She recently received the "alternate Nobel Prize" given by the Swedish Parliament to human rights activists.

Mariam Mar'i teaches at Haifa University and is the general director of the Early Childhood Educational Center for the Arab Child in Acre.

Haidar Abdel Shafi is a retired medical doctor and chairman of the Red Crescent Society in Gaza.

Leah Shakdiel is a religious feminist in Israel. She is also active in the New Israel Fund.

Ziad Abu Zayad is a lawyer and editor of the Palestinian newspaper in Hebrew, *Gesher*. He is currently in jail; Israeli authorities incarcerated him under the administrative detention decree.